HOW TO PLAN & REMODEL
ATTICS & BASEMENTS

*Created and designed by
the editorial staff of
ORTHO BOOKS*

Project Editor
Karin Shakery

Writer
Robert J. Beckstrom

Illustrators
Ron Hildebrand
Frank Hildebrand
Ronda Hildebrand

Ortho Books

Publisher
Robert L. Iacopi

Editorial Supervisor
Robert J. Dolezal

Production Director
Ernie S. Tasaki

Managing Editors
Anne Coolman
Michael D. Smith
Sally W. Smith

System Manager
Leonard D. Grotta

National Sales Manager
Charles H. Aydelotte

Marketing Specialist
Susan B. Boyle

Operations Coordinator
Georgiann Wright

Office Assistant
Marie Ongsiaco

Senior Technical Analyst
J. A. Crozier, Jr.

Chevron

Chevron Chemical Company
575 Market Street, San Francisco, CA 94105

Acknowledgments

Copy Chief
Melinda Levine

Copyeditor
Loralee Windsor

Editorial Assistant
Teri Lammers

Proofreader
Rebecca Pepper

Composition and Pagination
William F. Yusavage

Production Coordinator
Linda M. Bouchard

Photo Editor
Cindy Putnam

Production Artists
Deborah Cowder
Lezlly Freier
Anne Pederson

Indexer
Elinor Lindheimer

Photographs

Peter Aaron, Esto Photographics, Inc., back cover, pages 64, 65
Russell Abraham, pages 22, 23, 27, 31
Cotten Alston, pages 60–61, 66, 67
Laurie Black, pages 24, 49
Karen Bussolini, pages 29, 48, 62, 79
California Redwood Assn., pages 68, 80
Saxon Holt, pages 20–21
Wolfgang Hoyt, Esto Photographics, Inc., page 63
Michael LaMotte, page 9
Fred Lyon, pages 4–5, 7, 14
Stephen Marley, pages 9, 25, 26, 28, 68, 80
Kit Morris, pages 58–59
Kenneth Rice, page 69
Rion Rizzo, page 30
Durston Saylor, page 83
Velux-America, Inc., pages 30, 39

Designers & architects

Eric A. Chase, Branford, Conn., page 48
Elaine Class, Los Altos, Calif., page 23
Thomas F. Collum, Atlanta, Ga., page 30
Joyce Darrow, San Francisco, Calif., page 69
Syd Dunton/Trident Designs, Saratoga, Calif., page 68, 80
Joseph Durso, N.Y., NY, back cover, pages 64, 65
Jean Brown and Associates, Burlingame, Calif., page 31
Richard Gordon, N.Y., NY, page 63
Vivian Irvine, Burlingame, Calif., page 27
Lydon, Lynch Associates, Wolfville, N.S., Canada, page 39
Dan Phipps & Associates, San Francisco, Calif., pages 22, 24, 25, 28, 49
Andrew Robinson and Marsden Moran, Woodbridge, Conn., pages 62, 79
Rhoda Russota ASID and Rosalyn Cama ASID, Interior Design Associates, New Haven, Conn., page 29
L. Ward Seymour, Atlanta, Ga., pages 60, 61, 66, 67
Shope Reno Wharton Associates, Greenwich, Conn., front cover, page 83
Gail Steuart Woolaway ASID & Associates Sausalito, Calif., pages 58–59
Sandra York, San Francisco, Calif., page 26

Special thanks

California Redwood Assn.
Claire Carter
Don Eyrich, Marick Builders
Michael Hamman
Jeff Maddock, Marick Builders
Steve Needy, King Builders
Bill Simpson
Velux-America, Inc.
Ventarama Skylight Corp.
Sandra and Dan Webster
Bill Zimmerman

Front cover. A row of skylights provides height, light, and a view of the trees for this attic kitchen, dining, and living area. Photograph by Durston Saylor.

Back cover. A solarium transforms a dark basement into a sunlit garden room in which to tend plants or relax with a book.

Title page. Deeply textured walls and French doors opening onto a small balcony romanticize this room at the top.

HOW TO PLAN & REMODEL
ATTICS & BASEMENTS

PLANNING TO REMODEL

Converting a bare attic or basement into a pleasant living space should be an enjoyable experience. It involves seeing your dreams and ideas become a reality as you create environments that will suit your family's needs.

A conversion is a big project. Doing it well involves much more than nailing some plywood to the attic floor joists, rolling out a carpet, and moving in the furniture. You will be faced with a lot of planning and work unless you expect nothing more of a recreation room than the existing basement with painted walls and a table-tennis arrangement.

For the project to run smoothly and for the space to suit your budget as well as your desires and needs, it must be planned carefully and coordinated skillfully. Unless you are planning to do all the work yourself, you will be dealing with a lot of people who will have a myriad of questions that you must be prepared to answer quickly and accurately.

Before you plunge into planning, designing, and building your project, you must focus on some practical issues first. These lay the groundwork for everything else that comes ahead.

A smooth and efficient remodeling project is usually the result of careful planning and organizing. Being well prepared enables you to avert problems rather than having to solve them halfway through the construction process.

PRACTICAL CONSIDERATIONS

One of the first questions you need to answer is whether any type of conversion is legally permissible. Certain home improvements may be subject to regulations laid down by your local building department, planning commission, or neighborhood association. Your property deed may also contain restrictions.

Because attic and basement conversions involve existing space, they are seldom totally prohibited. But there may be limitations on the way they are used. For example, a separate apartment may not be allowed. There may also be restrictions placed on changes to the exterior, and the installation of a new dormer window may not be allowed.

The quickest way to find out if you will run into any problems is to phone or visit your local planning commission or building department. Explain that you are considering an attic or basement conversion and need to know if special restrictions apply.

If you live in a subdivision or an area with a neighborhood association, check to see if any type of conversion is subject to CCRs (Conditions, Covenants, and Restrictions), design review, or similar regulations. Finally, make sure that the deed to your property includes any clauses pertinent to remodeling.

These preliminary inquiries may save you valuable planning time should you discover any serious prohibitions. You can also find out what is involved in obtaining a variance if you feel your project merits a special exception to any regulations.

Budget

"How much will it cost?" is the question most people ask first, but more important is the question, "How much can I afford?"

To answer this question you need more than a quick look at your bank-account balance. For a realistic answer, you need to know:

☐ Your total net worth
☐ Anticipated new expenses (a baby, a car, college expenses)
☐ Your expected cash flow during the design and construction phases (and afterwards if you obtain a loan)
☐ Your borrowing power

You will not know your actual borrowing power until you apply and qualify for a loan, but your balance sheet will give you a pretty good idea. As well as a financial balance sheet, the lender will want your credit history and the assessed value of your home, if it will be used as security.

Once you determine your net worth and borrowing power, you can ask the question, "How much money am I willing to commit to either an attic or basement conversion?"

The answer depends largely on what such a conversion is really worth. The value of your home won't necessarily increase by the amount of money spent on improvements. The value is largely determined by the area in which you live. Consult with a local real-estate agent to determine the value of homes in your neighborhood and how much your home might be worth after the conversion project. For a more precise estimate, arrange for a professional appraisal (which will be required, anyway, if you apply for a home loan).

By comparing the current value of your home with its potential value, you will have a good idea of how much money to devote to improvements. If you love your home and neighborhood and plan to stay, spend whatever it takes—even though you might not recover your costs should you have to sell. If you are not so attached, it might be better to invest your resources in a larger home rather than adding new living space to your present one.

Determining your budget

To figure your net worth, follow the steps listed below.

1. Total your assets (cash, savings accounts, checking accounts, stocks, bonds, securities, surrender value of life insurance, market value of real estate, automobiles, furnishings, jewelry, pension funds, etc.).

2. Total your liabilities (real estate loans, accounts and contracts payable, installment loans, etc.).

3. Subtract your total liabilities from your total assets to find your net worth. This is the amount of assets you can liquidate into cash or pledge as security for a loan.

To figure out your monthly cash flow, do the following arithmetic.

1. Total your current monthly income (gross wages less withholding, investment income, monthly value of health and other benefits).

2. Total your current monthly expenses (mortgages, auto loans, property taxes, insurance payments, installment and credit-card payments, living expenses, etc.).

3. Subtract expenses from income to get your net monthly cash flow.

4. Project your net monthly cash flow for the next five years by adding any expected new income and subtracting any anticipated new expenses. Be sure to include new monthly expenses that will be incurred by your conversion, such as heating and electrical costs, increased insurance or taxes, and new furnishing payments.

5. Average your current and projected net monthly cash flow to obtain a realistic estimate of how much money will be available every month to pay back a new loan.

Practical needs

Budget is not the only factor that sets the limits of a project. Equally important are your needs and expectations. One of the most important questions of any remodeling project is one that is asked all too seldom: Why are we doing this?

Clarify your priorities. A successful conversion is designed for specific needs. Begin by thinking about your home as it is now. Imagine all the ways it could be improved, all the ways you could use extra space, and all the ways your existing space could be enhanced. Create a wish list—all the things you would like to have. Then prioritize your wishes.

You may discover that an attic or basement conversion does not even address the most important issues and is not as urgent a project as you had thought. Your list may also suggest other ways to use your attic or basement than you had originally planned. Most importantly, when you work with design professionals, these lists will enable them to provide better assistance.

Establish your level of commitment. How important is this project to you and to your family? How much time, money, and effort do you want to spend (number of hours per week)? When you answer, consider the activities that you are willing to give up for a while and the type of life-style you are willing to endure while your project is being designed and built.

Decide on the scope. Even before you begin a design you can make some important decisions about your project. Are you just finishing some walls and ceilings in the basement or are you getting involved in a major restructuring of the house? Do you want something really special, or just adequate? Do you have other options, such as converting the garage or building an addition? The answers will affect how much professional help will be necessary and what work you must do yourself.

Before getting too deeply immersed in your remodeling plans, do some careful thinking. Be sure that what you want coincides with the amount of time and money that you are willing to invest.

DESIGN

I f you have answered the practical questions previously discussed, you are ready to proceed with the design process.

Many people associate the word design with wallcoverings, floor coverings, trim details, light fixtures, and so on, or with magazine pictures of award-winning homes. But design can be simply your needs and preferences summarized on paper. Every project—whether large or small and involving professionals or novices—should be designed, that is, well-thought through.

The design process

The design process is the most critical and challenging phase of the entire project. It spans the distance between your dreams and the final set of working drawings. It defines what the space will look and feel like and how well it will work.

A good design determines how smoothly the construction and management phases of your project will go. An effective design reduces the chance of costly setbacks and surprises. It assures that bids are more accurate and contracts, more precise. It makes scheduling easier and helps settle, if not prevent, disputes. Good design inspires the builder and sets the tone for the entire project.

What makes a good design?

Many factors contribute to the success of a project, but the most important one is a thorough and carefully planned process.

Architects and professional designers know the process well. Their projects may seem to be the result of inspired creativity—and they often are—but they are also the product of a patient search for the best solutions to each design problem. The success of this search depends on the thoroughness of the process, the accuracy with which design problems are identified, and the ability to apply sound design criteria to solve them.

It is too easy to think of design as a minor nuisance to contend with before getting to the important and exciting steps, such as completing the project and moving in. However, many professionals estimate that proper design and planning represent more than one third of the work in any remodeling project. It is often the most exciting step, but it must also be done thoroughly and well.

There is no substitute for good design. The finest materials and best construction techniques will not cover up faulty design, and no project will go smoothly and stay within budget if the design is incomplete. All too often do-it-yourself remodelers (some professionals, too) encounter obstacles, setbacks, and surprises that could have been avoided with careful planning. As a homeowner, you play a major role in the design process. Depending on the scope of the project and the level to which you want to be involved, professional help may be needed. Often professionals can help you get what you want faster, better,

and cheaper. Do not assume that you will automatically save money by doing either the design or the construction work yourself.

On the other hand, do not assume that professionals know what you want better than you do, that your tastes will be the same, or that any professional will do. As a homeowner you have a tremendous advantage: You know how your home functions and how you would like it to function. You can test ideas by visualizing them as you carry on with day-to-day living. You know your family's needs and the shortcomings, as well as the assets, of your house. It is important to communicate all this information to the professional and to stay involved in the process.

If you want to plan the space yourself, be sure you know why. If it's because you enjoy designing, do as much of it yourself as possible, with occasional consultation from a professional to ensure that you are on the right track. If it's to save money, use the guidelines for choosing a professional to see where you save the most. If you feel design is not important enough to merit professional input, you may be underestimating the potential of your project. If you do not know how to work with design professionals, read the guidelines on pages 10–11.

Capturing a spirit

Every home and every room in it has a "feel," an overall character that you are aware of when you first enter. You may not know what creates it, but you do sense it and try to define it with words like restful, spacious, dramatic, dull, cluttered, vibrant, comfortable, or even contemporary, country, or Mediterranean.

Your attic or basement will have such a quality, too, although sometimes character is strongly affected by both structure and function. Perhaps you want the space to be bright and sunny, or cozy and dimly lit, or maybe you want it to resemble a country inn you once stayed at or a magazine photograph you like.

The overall feeling of a space is not just a detail that is added to a room like frosting on a cake; it is the creative integration of many different elements. You are more likely to capture it when you define it early in the design process and consider the definition when solving design problems.

The easiest way to begin defining the feeling you want to achieve is by looking through books and magazines. Clip out pictures, focus on details, observe homes that you visit, and keep notes of your impressions. You are not necessarily looking for spaces that you can duplicate but for ones that appeal to you and make you feel comfortable.

You might find that you are attracted to several different styles; that could happen because you will be paying attention to good design and not to a particular look. These apparent contradictions will help you and a designer identify the elements that you want to incorporate into your attic or basement design.

Keep track of details that you admire, even if a complete space is not appealing. Collect all this information and keep it in one place, such as a loose-leaf binder or a folder. Have it ready to refer to at meetings with architects and designers.

Appropriate materials for furnishing either an attic or basement are ones that will serve your functional needs as well as create the desired effect.

HIRING PROFESSIONALS

Because no two remodeling projects are the same, there are no hard-and-fast rules about hiring professionals. The type of person you should employ will vary according to your own needs and preferences.

Design is the most important phase of your project, so do not hesitate to hire professionals if you need help. You may have firm ideas about what you would like and only need someone to draft a set of working plans for a permit or construction bidding. On the other hand, you may want to engage professional help from the outset to help and guide you through the entire process. If your needs fall somewhere between these extremes, you can arrange periodic consultations with an architect or other specialist, such as a structural engineer, an interior designer, or a solar expert.

Your choice of professionals will depend on the scope of the job and the quality of design you desire. If the space is already structurally feasible and needs only finishing, then hire an interior designer. If the space needs structural modification or is large enough for several rooms, hire an architect or design/build contractor. If you need preliminary planning advice, hire an architect, engineer, or general contractor with experience in attic or basement conversions.

General contractors. General contractors are responsible for coordinating the various construction phases and supplying the personnel needed to complete a project according to a set of plans and at an agreed-upon price. In most states, contractors must be licensed, which certifies that they have had a specific amount of experience and, sometimes, that they have passed a test.

Although most contractors are not licensed or trained to do design work, some have the skills and experience necessary to help plan an attic or basement conversion. If plans submitted for approval to your building department must be drawn by an architect or engineer, you or your contractor can hire the appropriate professional on an hourly basis.

Design/build contractors. Some contracting firms, known as design/build contractors, have architects or building designers on staff or available as subcontractors. These companies will assume full legal responsibility from the beginning to the end of a project.

You will forgo the advantages of having competitive bids, but you will be working closely with one group of professionals who can coordinate their services in your best interest.

Architects. Architects are trained specifically and extensively in building design and engineering. Their skills include a concern for practicalities and details, and refined building techniques.

Most states have licensing requirements that include architectural schooling, a degree, and a certain number of years' experience. The American Institute of Architects offers the designation "AIA" to architects who meet its standards, which are often more stringent than state licensing requirements.

An architect provides planning and designing services and can manage your project from beginning through construction, acting as an arbiter in matters concerning you and the contractor. Sometimes architects will work on an hourly basis to provide consulting services for owner-builders.

Building designers. Building designers often have a training similar to that of an architect and in most states must be licensed. The American Institute of Building Designers offers the "AIBD" designation to designers who have at least two years of architectural training, have worked six years under the supervision of a licensed designer, and have passed stringent tests. In many states, building designers are limited in the kinds of projects they may undertake. Services provided are normally the same as those offered by architects.

Interior designers. Interior designers are experienced in coordinating all the finish elements that give a room its final look. They have access to decorator showrooms and products that the general public cannot normally find or buy.

Many states do not require a license, but membership in professional societies ensures a certain level of training and experience.

Some designers are independents, some work through design studios, and others offer services through a home-furnishings store.

If your attic or basement conversion involves only finishing the interior space, with no structural or exterior changes, you may want to work exclusively with an interior designer. If you plan to employ other design professionals, include the interior designer at the very beginning.

Specialized consultants. Some design consultants specialize in certain fields, such as lighting, telecommunications, solar energy, and kitchen design, or designs for children, allergy sufferers, or the disabled.

In most cases you are best able to use the services of consultants if you already have a preliminary plan that they can critique and improve upon.

Finding the right designer

When contracting for design work, you can find possible candidates from the following sources.

☐ Recommendations from friends, neighbors, and colleagues
☐ Listings in the Yellow Pages
☐ Newspaper listings
☐ Trade associations, such as the American Institute of Architects, American Institute of Building Designers, National Association of the Remodeling Industry, National Remodelers Institute, and American Society of Interior Designers
☐ Trade shows
☐ Home shows

Once you have gathered some names, make a few phone calls. Be ready to give a brief description of your project and to ask questions about the contractor's availability, references, and similiar experiences.

After following up references by visiting the projects and interviewing previous clients, there will probably be two or three professionals that you want to meet. At these meetings discuss your project further and try to get a sense of how well you will be able to work with these people and whether they will be able to meet your design needs. Once you have decided upon which person you would prefer to work with, you are ready to draw up a contract.

Drawing up contracts

Because design is an open-ended process that involves give and take, it is important to have a clear, written contract for any work beyond an hourly consultation.

Most professionals have a standard contract form. Review it together carefully and be sure that it includes a payment schedule, specifies what drawings will be furnished, guarantees that the final design will meet codes, and provides a preliminary cost estimate for completing the remodeling project.

Before signing a contract, consult with an attorney about any clauses that are unclear or ones that make you feel uncomfortable.

Working with professionals

The amount of time needed for the design process will vary from hours for a brief consultation to months for changing and refining dozens of ideas. But the better prepared you are before meeting with design professionals, the more they will be able to help you.

For your first meeting, have ready your budget; your priority list of needs and desires; any drawings, sketches, or other documents relating to your home; and a file of clippings or photographs that might be helpful.

Throughout the process be prepared to clarify, to disagree, to consider alternatives to your ideas, and to make firm decisions. For their part, professionals that you are dealing with should be willing to listen to your needs, commit to and meet all deadlines, and provide you with a design that meets your budget requirements.

Saving money

Payment for professional advice is money well spent. It can even reduce cost in the long run. This is often the case in the following situations.

☐ When you are working with a very tight budget and you need a design that will result in an efficient, economical space
☐ When you have particular ideas in mind and need help in drawing them up
☐ When you need advice about structural changes or ways to fulfill code requirements
☐ When you need drawings of the basic plan so other professionals, such as an interior designer or lighting consultant, can assist you most effectively
☐ When you require a permit for your project or if you are opening it to bids
☐ When you have seen work you admire and want to duplicate it

GETTING READY TO BUILD

Translating your design into a finished space is an exciting as well as demanding phase of your project. Even if you hire others to do all of the work, you still will play a major role in the process.

The three keys to ensuring a smooth construction phase are:
☐ A complete and thorough set of plans and elevations
☐ Selection of the right professionals
☐ Realistic assessment of your own capabilities, if you plan to do any of the work yourself

Construction documents

You may have selected a contractor that you already know and respect to do your project, or you may be planning to be your own general contractor. If you do not have a particular contractor in mind, you need a complete set of construction documents, as outlined on page 14, to submit your project to bid.

Soliciting bids

You should observe a certain etiquette when soliciting bids. If you are working with an architect or designer, this person will most likely handle the bidding process, even though the final selection is up to you. If you are obtaining the bids yourself, observe these guidelines.
☐ Do not undertake a formal bid process if you already have a contractor in mind. Just negotiate directly.
☐ In your initial phone call to each contractor, describe the project briefly and mention that complete plans are available.
☐ Have a list of questions ready about the contractor's similiar experiences, method of scheduling construction, and references.
☐ Check references by visiting job sites and completed projects. Ask previous clients if they were satisfied with the contractor's performance and attitude.
☐ Narrow your choices to three to six people, and provide each with a complete set of plans.
☐ Set a firm date for receiving bids, allowing at least two weeks if the cost is likely to exceed $10,000 or if there will be several subcontractors.
☐ If a bidder requests clarification or further information, answer the request in writing and send a copy, labeled "Addendum," to each one of the contractors that are bidding.
☐ Use the same addendum process for any changes you make in the plans after they have been submitted for bids.
☐ Along with the price quote, request a copy of the contract form that the bidder expects you to sign, and bank or credit references.
☐ Review the bids carefully.

Selecting a contractor

The selection of a contractor should be based on the following factors.
☐ Your feelings (the person whose work you like best, who seems most appropriate for the size and type of job, and whose personality meshes best with your own)
☐ Schedules (yours and theirs)
☐ Cost (a low bid is not necessarily the one to choose; it may be an indication of poor-quality work, minimal supervision, or costly changes later on)

It is unethical to negotiate simultaneously with two contractors after you have received bids, or to invite another contractor to compete after the bidding process closes. Remember to notify all parties of your choice and the winning bid price, and thank them for taking time to bid.

Signing the contract

Always insist on a well-written contract. It does not have to be elaborate; since most contractors already have their own contract form, you can use it as a starting point. Not all of the following provisions will apply to your situation, but a good contract should include these points.

☐ Reference to the construction documents as the criteria of performance
☐ Stipulation that all permits are to be obtained by the contractor and all work done according to code
☐ Specified start and completion dates and a detailed schedule
☐ Clear delineation between contractor's supervisory duties and yours
☐ Specification of the work that you intend to perform yourself
☐ A list of all materials or fixtures you will be supplying
☐ A payment schedule corresponding to key completion dates
☐ A provision for the contractor to supply lien releases from all subcontractors and suppliers before final payment is made
☐ Requirements for final payment, including a final inspection by your building department, a certificate of completion by you and the architect, and a 30-day waiting period
☐ A certificate of insurance from the contractor covering all risks, with you as a named beneficiary
☐ Specific procedures for handling change orders
☐ Specific procedures for communication when there is more than one professional involved
☐ A method for resolving disputes

Legalities

In most communities you will be required to obtain a building permit before starting construction. Usually the homeowner is allowed to apply for the permit, but in some communities permits may only be issued to licensed contractors. Once the plans are submitted, it may take a few weeks for them to be checked and approved. You can probably have the permit issued immediately if you are only finishing or making minor changes to existing interior space.

Separate permits are customarily issued for the building, plumbing, electrical, and mechanical stages in a remodeling project.

Besides complying with the law, a permit confers several advantages. It validates any work done that affects the home's resale value. It decreases the possibility that an insurance company would refuse a claim against fire or other damage on the basis of its dubious origin. It also provides an incentive for thorough planning and design and for a sense of pride in your work. Finally, and most importantly, codes and permits exist to ensure that you and your family will be living in a safe home.

Inspections. Your permit will include a schedule of inspections. As a rule, the inspector will check each phase of the job just before it is covered over with concrete, wallboard, or any other material that makes it impossible to evaluate the quality of materials and workmanship. A typical schedule of necessary inspections appears below.

Your contractor will call for inspections and be responsible for answering questions, although you may have to make arrangements to let the inspector onto the premises if the contractor is not there.

Most inspectors are more than willing to answer questions about their interpretation of the code or their inspection of the work. However, they may not advise you on how to do something. If you are not sure if the work will meet code, ask a professional builder who knows the local codes to take a look first.

Code compliance. When you do an attic or basement conversion, codes usually apply only to the new work. The building department generally does not expect you to bring your entire home up to current standards unless the building inspector finds a hazardous situation. Some existing conditions in plumbing, electrical wiring, and stairs, for example, may be governed by current codes, but most features of your home are governed by the codes applicable at the time of construction.

If your are doing an extensive amount of plumbing and wiring in an older home, it would make sense to modernize your systems, even if this is not required by code. Spending a little more money now can save a lot of additional expense later.

Inspections

Job	Work to be checked	Time of inspection
Foundation	Trench, forms, rebar	Before concrete is poured
Under the floor	Floor framing, utility lines	Before subfloor is installed
Framing	Grade of lumber, connections	Before sheathing is applied
Sheathing	Seams, nailing patterns	Before roofing or siding
Rough plumbing	Pipe sizes, materials	Before plumbing is covered
Rough wiring	Wire size, boxes, workmanship	Before wiring is covered
Roofing	Materials, flashing	After roofing is completed
Energy efficiency	Insulation, window area	Before applying wallboard
Interior walls	Wallboard nailing pattern	Before taping and mudding
Flues/fireplace	Clearances, materials	Before covering
Gas line	Fittings, pressure test	Before covering
Final inspection	Electrical fixtures, plumbing fixtures, railings, furnace smoke detectors	After completion

One of the most useful tools for designing new space is a floor plan. It indicates dimensions, wall locations, window placements, stairs, and other physical features. As you consider various design issues, the floor plan will go through several phases of changes and refinements—each change making the space more livable and enjoyable.

Not all projects require plans. If you are covering a floor or installing some paneling, the process will simply consist of choosing the materials. If you are hiring a plumber to move a fixture, no plans will be necessary. But if the project is extensive or involves structural and mechanical changes, the design process will require a formal set of working plans to be used for itemizing materials, estimating costs, getting bids, obtaining permits, and guiding construction.

How detailed should plans be?

As you work with a floor plan, remember that the actual space you are planning is three-dimensional. The ceiling, walls, furnishings, fixtures, and windows create forms and surfaces that have enormous impact. Always ask yourself what it would feel like to be inside the planned space.

How detailed and extensive should your plans be? Basically, the more money you want to save, the more detailed your plans should be. This tends to be true even if you intend to do all the work yourself. There are several reasons for that.

☐ Detailed plans ensure accurate bids by contractors, minimizing the likelihood of unrealistic estimates or costly misunderstandings.

☐ Detailed plans are essential in order to get competitive bidding, a time-honored process that works in the owner's favor.

☐ Drafting plans requires thinking through every detail. The more effort spent at the pencil-and-paper stage, the fewer costly changes later on.

☐ If you are doing the work yourself, detailed plans will make you more efficient and better prepared.

☐ Itemizing all materials and fixtures will make it easier to shop around for the best prices.

Final plans and specifications

If you require a complete set of plans, they should include working drawings, specification and materials lists, and a statement of general conditions. These documents are used to itemize materials, estimate costs, obtain bids and permits, and guide construction. If the plans are complete and thorough, the project should move smoothly to completion.

An attic conversion is likely to require more extensive documents than a basement, especially if the plan involves changes to the exterior or to the floor and roof framing. Full documents include the following items.

Floor plan

This plan shows walls, doors, windows, stairs, closets, built-ins, hidden spaces, possible furniture arrangement, plumbing fixtures, electrical outlets, lights, existing obstacles, and dimensions. First-floor and foundation plans may also be required in the case of an attic remodeling.

Section drawings

These are drawings that show structural conditions, the stairwell, and, in the case of an attic conversion, they will also include the roof slope.

Materials lists

These lists include all materials necessary for framing. These include insulation; wall, roof, and floor coverings; beams; posts; foundation piers; skylight and dormer framing (for an attic); and all dimensions.

Framing plan

For an attic conversion, you may have to submit a plan that shows floor joists or roof rafters for any new framing, beams, and headers.

Interior elevations

Interior elevations are drawings for each of the four walls in all rooms that show surface materials, dimensions, built-ins, windows, doors, trim details, hardware, outlets, fixtures, furnishings, and colors and fabrics, where appropriate.

Specification lists

These include framing lumber, trim lumber, millwork, floor coverings, wallcoverings, windows, doors, hardware, fixtures.

Statement of general conditions

This document describes expected level of workmanship, specific details or items that are essential to the project, and performance criteria.

Your remodeling plans will progress from doodles, rough sketches, and final sketches showing electrical circuits to a full set of working plans.

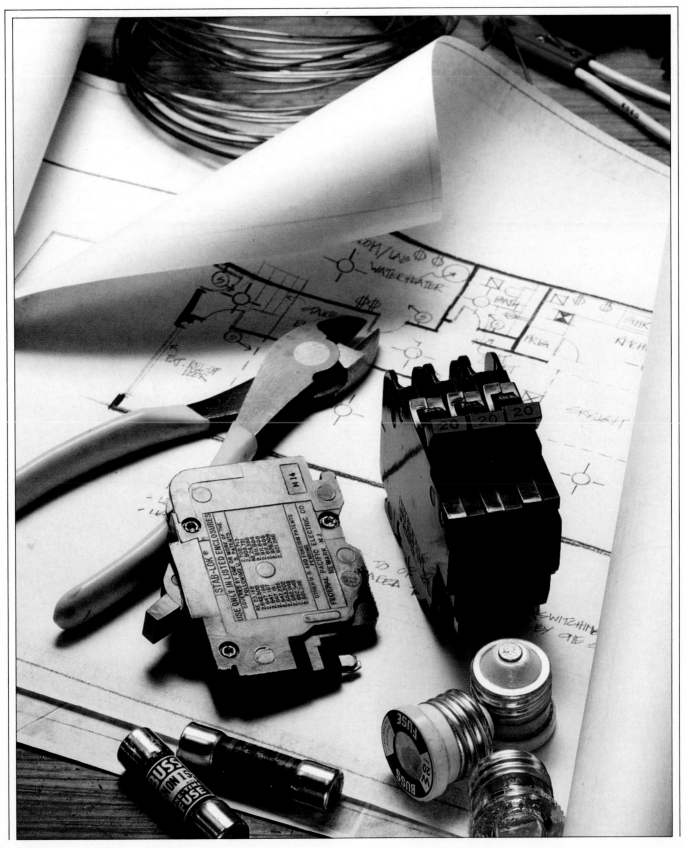

DOING IT YOURSELF

There are many things you may be able to do yourself. On the other hand, taking full responsibility for a major remodeling will involve a lot of time and effort. It may also result in additional expense if you do not already own a comprehensive collection of tools. Be honest in assessing your own skills and, even more importantly, the amount of time and effort you are prepared to invest.

Will doing it yourself save you money?

There is no guarantee that doing a sizable remodeling project yourself will save money, especially if you put a monetary value on your time. However, the following guidelines can help you to cut costs.

☐ Do the work of the highest paid professionals (usually plumbers and electricians).

☐ Do tasks with a high labor cost relative to materials cost, such as demolition, excavation, wallboard finishing, insulating, and concrete work.

☐ Do small jobs that would take a subcontractor less than a half day to perform, such as installing vinyl flooring in a bathroom or kitchen.

☐ Take responsibility for buying and delivering all materials to the job.

Questions to ask yourself

Before you decide how much of the conversion you are going to do yourself, read through the following questionnaire and answer truthfully.

Managing the project
Are you well organized, persistent, clear about the details of your project, and able to spend long hours on the telephone and at the job? Can you handle money, make payments promptly, and keep a budget? Are you comfortable negotiating with subcontractors and suppliers? Are you articulate and patient?

Performing a trade
Are you experienced in a trade, such as carpentry or plumbing, or with a material: wallboard or paint? Do you have access to the proper tools? Are you willing to be assigned as a subcontractor by the builder, and can you make yourself available whenever necessary, have materials ready, and complete work as scheduled?

Doing general labor
Are there significant amounts of demolition, excavation, or materials hauling that you can do before others take over the job? Are you available on short notice to assist with menial tasks? Can such tasks be specified clearly enough in the contract for a clear delineation between your and the contractor's responsibility?

Doing it all yourself
Do you enjoy working on your home? Do you have time? Will the project disrupt normal day-to-day living? Will it matter if the project remains unfinished for several months? Have you finished every project you ever started?

Being your own contractor

You may want to manage the job yourself and hire specialists—plumbers, electricians, concrete workers, wallboard finishers, painters, and tilers—to do the actual work.

Obligations
Although you will be hiring professionals, you will still have certain roles and responsibilities, such as being thoroughly familiar with the contract and construction documents. You must also be financially sound and able to make prompt payments. Be friendly but stay out of the way. Direct all inquiries, complaints, or compliments to the general contractor or to the person with whom you signed the contract.

Documents
If there is not a formal set of plans, the contractor should submit a sketch outlining the proposed work before you sign a contract.

Ask to see proof of workers' compensation insurance from any subcontractors. Also, be sure to obtain lien releases from all subcontractors and suppliers before making your final payment.

Staying on schedule
Subcontractors depend on accurate scheduling. If your job is not ready when they arrive, you may not see them again for several days or even weeks until they can reschedule your job. Keep all subcontractors informed of any suspected delays.

Salaried labor
You should not hire workers or unlicensed professionals unless you are willing to take on the responsibilities of an employer. Obviously this does not apply to members of your own family. The responsibilities of an employer include reporting wages to the IRS, withholding taxes, and carrying workers' compensation insurance.

Preparing for construction

A remodeling project inevitably causes disruptions and mess. Water turned off at the wrong time can be annoying; the lack of a door, inconvenient; the loss of a staircase, nerve-wracking. The more familiar you are with the plans and the schedule, the better you will be able to cope.

If you are going to do some of the work yourself, there are steps that you can do ahead of time.

☐ Clear out the area where you will be working. This may involve a yard sale or a major reorganization of household goods, so start early.

☐ Plan how you will dispose of debris. Collect cardboard boxes for carrying out plaster and broken concrete. Inquire about rental rates for a dumpster or a truck. Clear out an area of your yard for dumping dirt.

☐ Place orders early for materials that require time for delivery.

☐ Arrange for the covered storage of materials that will be delivered.

☐ Inventory your tools. Organize them for quick access. Replace any broken tools. Buy safety goggles, gloves, and dust masks.

Checklist for you, the client

☐ Determine from the building department whether there are restrictions.

☐ Establish a budget.

☐ Inquire about a loan.

☐ Clarify your priorities, level of commitment, and the scope of the project.

☐ Contact design professionals.

☐ Interview and check references of candidates.

☐ Select design professionals.

☐ Review and sign design contract.

☐ Design the project.

☐ Obtain final plans and construction documents.

☐ Obtain financing.

☐ Submit plans for permits.

☐ Contact construction professionals.

☐ Interview and check references of candidates.

☐ Solicit bids.

☐ Select contractor(s).

☐ Review and sign construction contracts.

☐ Obtain permits.

☐ Schedule all subcontractors.

Checklist for you, the contractor

☐ Perform demolition.

☐ Perform basic structural work on doors, windows, stairs, exterior, etc.

☐ Arrange for rough wiring, plumbing, and mechanical work.

☐ Arrange inspections, as needed.

☐ Install insulation.

☐ Install and tape wallboard.

☐ Buy all finish fixtures.

☐ Install trim and interior doors.

☐ Paint.

☐ Install flooring in bathroom and kitchen.

☐ Install cabinets, shelves; finish plumbing and electrical fixtures, etc.

☐ Install main flooring.

☐ Arrange for final inspection, file notice of completion and (if required), obtain lien releases.

☐ Make final payments.

GLOSSARY OF TERMS

Attic terms

Bearing wall. A wall that supports floor loads or roof loads, with support underneath it directly connected to the foundation.

Bird's mouth. A notch cut into a rafter so it can rest on the house wall.

Collar tie. A horizontal board nailed between two rafters to keep them from spreading apart.

Curb. A frame for holding a skylight above the roof.

Dormer. An extension of attic space jutting out from the main roof.

Drop ceiling. A ceiling, supported by its own framing system, dropped below the roof to provide a standard ceiling height for a room.

Eave. The area under a roof near the exterior house wall that is too low for living space. (See *Overhang*.)

Egress. A secondary escape route that is required for sleeping and living spaces in case of emergency.

Gable dormer. A dormer with a gable-style roof. Front wall is peaked.

Gable roof. The most common style of roof, consisting of two sloped roof planes joined at the top.

Gable wall. The peaked house wall at the end of a gable roof.

Glazing area. The total window and skylight area. Codes specify a minimum of 10 percent of the floor area and often a maximum allowable glazing area for energy conservation.

Gusset. A metal plate used to join together two members of a truss.

Headroom. The distance between finished floor and finished ceiling or other overhead obstruction. Codes require it to be at least 7'6" for habitable rooms, 7' for hallways and bathrooms, and 6'8" for doorways.

Heat stratification. The accumulation of warmer air near the roof and cooler air near the ground floor, resulting in the overheating of an attic. Paddle fans and special ducts with internal fans destratify the air.

Hip roof. A variation of the gable roof style that eliminates gable walls at the ends of the house, reducing usable space in the attic. Roof planes slope upward from all four walls, intersecting each other at right angles.

Joist. A horizontal framing member used to support a floor or ceiling.

Kneewall. A low wall, usually 4 to 5 feet high. In attics, kneewalls close off the eaves from the living space.

Load is the total amount of weight a structure can be expected to support. **Dead load** refers to the weight of the building components, normally calculated as 10 pounds per square foot for floors and roofs. **Live load** is the additional weight of furnishings, people, and factors such as snow, wind, or earthquake. Amount of permissible weight is normally 40 pounds per square foot for floors, and 15 pounds per square foot for roof loads.

Overhang. The section of roof extending beyond the walls of the house; sometimes called an *eave*.

Pitch. The angle of a roof, usually measured as the number of inches of vertical rise for each 12 inches of horizontal run (for example, 8 in 12). Also called *slope*.

Plates. The horizontal members of a stud wall. The *soleplate* is at the bottom; the *top plate* of a bearing wall is always made out of two horizontal members. It supports joists.

Purlin. Intermediate support for long rafters functioning as a beam.

Rafters are the main framing members that support the roof. **Common rafters** are full-length and support most of the roof. **Fly rafters** (also called *rake* or *barge* rafters) are located on the outside of the house walls. **Hip rafters,** forming the intersection between a hip section of roof and the regular gable roof, are sized larger than common rafters. **Jack rafters** are short and fill in the space between a hip rafter and the house wall or between a valley rafter and roof ridge. **Valley rafters** form the joint where two roof planes intersect to form a valley.

Ridge beam. A beam that supports the tops of rafters, which is required when pairs of rafters are not connected by collar ties or ceiling joists.

Ridge board. A 1-by board running the length of the roof, against which pairs of rafters abut.

Roofing. The weatherproofing material covering a roof, such as wood or composition shingles, metal panels, tile, or slate.

Roof window. Another term for skylight; often refers to skylights with flat, clear glass that can be opened.

Sheathing. Plywood or 1-by boards nailed to the tops of rafters to provide a continuous roof surface.

Shed dormer. A dormer with a rectangular, rather than peaked, front wall and a single roof plane.

Slope. See *Pitch*.

Soffit. An overhead, boxlike enclosure. On the exterior of the house, it is the material used to enclose the area beneath an overhanging roof eave. In interior spaces, it is a dropped section of ceiling that can conceal obstructions.

Stack. A 4-inch vertical pipe that serves as the main plumbing vent and drain for a bathroom.

Strongback. A framing member nailed above sagging ceiling joists to help support them, usually consisting of a 2 by 4 laid flat across the joists and a 2 by 8 nailed next to it on edge. Its presence in the attic indicates weak ceiling joists that will have to be strengthened before they can support an attic floor.

Struts. Upright framing members which support purlins.

Truss. A prefabricated roof framing unit used instead of conventional rafters, and consisting of light framing lumber connected by gussets.

Vapor barrier. Plastic sheeting or similar material applied to framing before wallboard is installed. It prevents moisture in the living space from penetrating into the wall or ceiling cavity where it may be condensed and trapped in cold weather.

Vent. A plumbing pipe that goes through the attic to the roof to allow sewer gases to escape and air to enter the plumbing system. It prevents siphoning of the P-traps.

Winders. Pie-shaped stair treads used where a stairway turns a corner. As the narrow ends can be a hazard, winders are not recommended.

Basement terms

Access panel. A removable panel for access to pipes, valves, cleanouts, and other concealed utility devices.

Adhesives. High-strength glues that usually come in tubes to be used with a caulking gun. Some are used for attaching subflooring to joists; some for attaching insulation of concrete walls; and some for installing wallboard, paneling, or mirrors.

Anchor bolts. Bolts that are embedded in the foundation wall to hold the sill in place.

Block wall. Foundation wall that is made from concrete blocks mortared together.

Column. A vertical structural member, usually steel or wood, for supporting a girder.

Crawl space. The unexcavated area under a house, usually with a dirt floor and not deep enough for a basement living space.

Cripple wall. A low wall between the foundation and first floor.

Dampproofing. A superficial sealing of basement walls when there are minor seepage problems. Materials commonly used are cement-based coatings, epoxy-based sealers, and rubber-based paints.

Daylight wall. A basement wall that is substantially above ground, on the downslope side of a house.

Downspout. Vertical pipe for carrying water down from the roof gutters.

Drain mat. A plastic grid or similar device placed against the exterior of a foundation wall to intercept water flowing toward the wall and divert it downward into the footing drain.

Drainpipe. Three- or four-inch-diameter pipe with holes on the sides for collecting underground seepage and carrying it away from a foundation. ABS, PVC, and vitrified clay are the most common materials.

Efflorescence. A powdery, white substance that forms on concrete or masonry walls, left by water seeping through the wall.

Footing. A concrete base for supporting a foundation wall or pier.

Foundation seal. Insulation or similar material placed between the top of a foundation wall and the wood sill for sealing out drafts, dust, and air infiltration.

Foundation wall. A concrete or masonry wall that supports the perimeter walls of the house, retains soil, and keeps wood structural members from direct contact with the soil.

Frost line. The lowest depth at which the ground can be expected to freeze in a local region. It determines the required minimum depth for foundation footings and basement wall insulation.

Furring strips. 1 by 2 boards attached to a foundation wall. These boards provide a nailing surface for the finish wall.

Girder. Main beam supporting the floor joists.

Grade. The surface of the ground.

Hydrostatic pressure. The pressure exerted upon basement walls and floors from large amounts of ground water.

Isolation joint. Made from special compressible material placed between a concrete slab and adjacent concrete mass, such as a basement wall, to allow the slab to expand.

Lally column. A steel post filled with concrete, used in basements to support heavy house loads.

Leader. An extension at the bottom of a downspout to carry rainwater away from the foundation.

Main drain. A 4-inch pipe for carrying waste from the plumbing system to the house sewer.

Mastic. An inexpensive adhesive for attaching material over a large surface area.

Parging. A cementitious mortar applied to the exterior of a foundation wall before it is backfilled.

Partition wall. Any interior wall; often a nonbearing wall used to define spaces.

Pier. A concrete or masonry footing, usually isolated from the rest of the foundation. The pier supports a post or column.

Polyethylene. A plastic sheeting material that is normally used for vapor barriers under concrete slabs or as a vapor barrier on insulated walls and ceilings.

Post. A vertical support.

Pressure-treated lumber. With preservatives injected into it under pressure, this type of lumber is used in foundation sills, soleplates in basement walls, and other applications where the wood may come into direct contact with concrete or masonry that touches the ground.

Rebar. Reinforcing steel for concrete and concrete block work.

Rigid insulation. Panels of insulating material usually composed of some plastic, such as extruded polystyrene or isocyanurate, but sometimes of fiberglass. Requires less space than blanket or loose insulation and can withstand some moisture.

Screed. A board used to level off the surface of concrete.

Sill. A 2-by board bolted to the top of a foundation wall for supporting the floor joists or a low cripple wall.

Slab. A concrete floor, usually 4 inches thick and reinforced with heavy wire mesh.

Sleepers. Boards, usually pressure-treated 2 by 4s, that are attached to a concrete slab for supporting a wood subfloor.

Sump. A pit in the lowest area of a basement floor for collecting water from the surface of the floor. The water is removed with a sump pump.

Suspended ceiling. A ceiling of acoustical tile panels laid into a metal grid hung from the floor joists above a basement.

Swale. A small valley or surface depression created to divert water around a house.

Termite guard. A continuous metal flashing between the foundation wall and sill to provide a barrier against termites climbing up to the wood portion of a home.

Waterproofing. Material applied to the exterior of a foundation wall, usually asphalt emulsion or bentonite, a clay substance.

NEW HEIGHTS FOR ATTICS

*A*n attic offers marvelous potential for extra living space that has excitement and appeal. It provides privacy and seclusion; the interesting rooflines create dramatic angles and shapes. Windows or skylights can make you feel closer to the sky—soaring above treetops, sleeping under the stars and moon, or watching the world go by beneath your private aerie. Attics can be warm and cozy places in the winter. In the summer they can be pleasantly cool if windows or vents are placed to catch breezes, and if one or two trees arch overhead to provide some shade.

Attics lend themselves well to many decorating styles: a charming country look; a contemporary space with sleek lines and uncluttered spaces; or a rustic room with exposed beams, natural wood paneling, and a crackling fire in a wood-burning stove. Whatever your decorating preferences, you can exercise your most creative talents on an attic conversion—with more freedom than you would have downstairs because the new space does not need to be integrated with the rest of the house.

Even if your attic is cramped and has a low roof, it has potential. You can build a dormer and raise part of the roof, or you can remove the downstairs ceiling and build a small loft under the roof ridge. And if the attic does not meet your needs for actual living, turn it into an efficient storage area and use the emptied downstairs closets as additional living space.

An attic room tucked into the peak of a shingled roof offers wonderful views of the surrounding trees and lush garden.

EXPLORING POSSIBILITIES

T*he photos and guidelines on the following ten pages illustrate various ways an attic can be used. Considering all the options will help you to clarify and prioritize your needs and give you ideas.*

Family rooms

Available space in some homes may be claimed for so many different purposes that there is no place where the entire family can gather. A new family room in the attic may be the answer. It can be shared by adults and children and used for informal entertaining. It can also be a center in which to assemble all your electronic entertainment equipment.

For a family room, consider:
☐ A cheery atmosphere with skylights or south-facing windows
☐ Comfortable seating for eight or more people (a space at least 10 feet square)
☐ Convenient access, for example, from the main entry if used for frequent entertaining
☐ Tables and counters for games, hobbies, and eating
☐ A quiet corner for a study desk
☐ A minikitchen or facilities for preparing light snacks, including a bar sink, refrigerator, small counter, and adequate wiring
☐ An outdoor balcony or deck to expand living space and provide an emergency exit
☐ An adjoining bathroom or one that is close to the stairs

If you plan to use an attic as a family room, it is often desirable to divide the total space into smaller areas for specific uses. A partition wall with a large opening cut into it will separate spaces without isolating them.

*When you want to open your own bar,
consider making the attic the spot to
serve aperitifs to dinner guests. And an
authentic Victorian bar, complete with
brass footrail and bench seating, will
accommodate the crowds that can be
expected on a sunny Sunday morning.*

Multipurpose rooms

If the attic space is limited or if you have many different needs to satisfy, you can use your new rooms for more than one purpose. For instance, you could combine a master suite with office space (although you might end up living most of your life in the attic). Or you could use the attic for an office that doubles as a guest room.

For a multipurpose room, consider:

☐ Flexible shelving and storage to house various pieces of equipment
☐ Cabinet doors to protect equipment and keep out the dust
☐ Plenty of electrical outlets
☐ Special wiring for speakers and cable hookups
☐ Comfortable seating where all TV viewers can see the screen at an angle no sharper than 45 degrees, from no farther away than 10 to 12 feet, and away from traffic paths
☐ Sound insulation in the floor and door, if necessary
☐ Windows guarded from direct sunlight or glare

Hobby rooms

Whether you want a sewing room, a studio for painting or weaving, a gallery for displaying a collection, a chamber for playing music, or a tower for meditating, your attic may be just the place.

For a hobby room, consider:

☐ Counter space to hold a sewing machine and spread out materials
☐ Whether you will need to carry large or heavy materials, canvases, and frames up and down the stairs
☐ Skylights and windows on the north side for indirect light
☐ Easy-to-clean surfaces, especially on counters and the floor
☐ A sink for washing brushes
☐ Ventilation to remove any noxious fumes caused by paint and glue
☐ Lockable storage to protect small children from dangerous materials

Above: *A desk and a sofa are backed up against the kneewalls in order to take full advantage of the lower-height space in this skylight-lit attic. Built-ins, such as bookcases, can be used to put all the odd-shaped alcoves to good use.*

Opposite: *The structural elements that determine the shape of an attic often result in an architecturally interesting room. Good light and plenty of counter space make it an ideal place in which to pursue a hobby such as sewing.*

Bedrooms

An attic can provide the space for an extra bedroom or even a suite. It offers seclusion, views, and an interesting space that lends itself to very personal decorating styles ranging from a romantic, old-fashioned boudoir to a space-age fantasy retreat. The alcoves and nooks of an attic create ideal sitting and storage spaces within the large room of a master suite. Or an attic can become a private space for teenagers.

The following are minimum clearances; whenever possible, allow more space:

42 inches along the side or at the foot of a bed for dressing

20 inches between the side of a double bed and the wall

40 inches in front of a closet or chest of drawers

4 to 5 linear feet of closet per person

24-inch closet depth

For any bedroom, consider:

☐ Whether the stairs are too awkward for the people who will be using or cleaning the room.

☐ Whether you can meet code requirements for the following: direct egress to the outside through a door or a window with an unobstructed opening of at least 5.7 square feet; a smoke alarm outside each bedroom and over the stairs; safe use of gas or kerosene appliances; adequate ventilation (usually an openable window area equal to one tenth of the bedroom floor area).

☐ An attic bathroom (or half bath).

☐ Street noise (adults are usually less tolerant than children).

☐ A laundry chute.

☐ A bedside telephone.

☐ Windows placed high on the wall (except where drafts or rain affect the space directly below) for more flexible furniture groupings.

☐ Exposure to the sun. West-facing bedrooms may make the room too hot; south-facing bedrooms are pleasant for daytime use; east-facing bedrooms will get morning sunlight.

Covering the walls with redwood adds warmth to a cozy attic bathroom and integrates the tile-topped counter. Boxed counters and benches are a simple way to obscure pipes and ducts that service a new bathroom or the rest of the house.

Honey-colored pine and white ruffled bed linens play up the romance of a bedroom in the eaves. Note how the soft curves of the willow tester bed and the top of the armoire repeat the arched shapes of the walls and ceiling.

For a master suite, consider:
☐ A sleeping area
☐ A luxury bathroom with large soaking tub and two sinks
☐ One or two large closets
☐ A reading or conversation area

For a teenager's bedroom, consider:
☐ A place to study with a desk, a comfortable chair, and good lighting
☐ A loft bed with storage underneath

For a child's bedroom, consider:
☐ Extra play or hobby space
☐ A space-saving bed, such as a bunk or trundle bed
☐ A deep window seat to serve as an extra bed for overnight guests
☐ Plenty of storage for toys, books, and games
☐ Storage bins on casters
☐ Table for drawing and painting. Make sure it is a comfortable height for your child
☐ Clothes closet with a hanging rail at a height a child can reach

Above: *If the windows are small or the view is un-appealing, create the illusion of a picture window wall by installing vertical blinds. Full-length blinds can also be used to cover surface irregularities or conceal pipes and ducts.*

Opposite: *A small dormer window can be enlarged to provide more daylight in an attic office. Here the window reflects the shape of the dormer and is framed in wood that matches the long, laminate-covered desk.*

Offices

An attic is an excellent space for an office. It is remote enough to make you feel as if you had you left home to get there, yet very convenient. It is a dramatic space for stimulating creativity or for meeting clients. It has plenty of space for concealed storage, and you can plan windows, sky-lights, walls, doors, lighting, and wiring around your work needs.

The following is a list of useful space requirements. These are minimums and, wherever possible, more space should be allowed:
64 square feet of floor area for desk, chair, file cabinet, and typing table
30-inch desk height
30-inch desk depth
8- to 12-inch shelf depth
26-inch-high typing/computer table
36-inch counter height
42 inches of space in front of a file cabinet
36 inches of space in front of a bookcase

For an office, consider:
☐ An outside entrance or stairs convenient to the front door for visitors and delivery
☐ Sound insulation from the stairwell, if necessary
☐ Comfortable seating for reading or conferences
☐ Direct lighting over work areas
☐ A business or use permit from your city, if required

Sunrooms

A sunroom or solarium is a pleasant way to heat part of your home with solar energy. However, unless you provide a means of circulating the air to other parts of the house, the sunlight will heat only the spaces in and adjacent to the sunroom.

Although a sunroom makes a pleasant sitting or workroom during the day, remember that it may not be usable on cold, winter nights.

For a sunroom, consider:
☐ A minimum of four hours of direct sunlight on December 22
☐ South-facing window area equal to about 15 percent of floor area
☐ Overhangs or shade covers to minimize overheating in the summer
☐ Insulating devices to minimize heat loss during winter nights
☐ Doors to close off the space from the rest of the house
☐ Overhead ventilation
☐ A faucet or drip irrigation system for watering plants
☐ Fabrics and furnishings that will resist fading and drying out

Large openable windows, cut into a sloped roof, make this gallery office a bright and airy place to study. And, if it gets too warm, work can be carried out onto the deck through the sliding glass doors off the landing.

Retreats

Crowded, busy homes need a small retreat where a member of the family can get away for some quiet time alone. The attic, perched above the rest of the world, is a perfect place for such a retreat. This is also a good use for attics too small for conventional living space.

Sometimes the attic can be converted into a loft. This will create an open, flowing space between the attic and downstairs areas, making the retreat feel less cramped.

If there is enough headroom in the attic, convert part of the space into a retreat and remove the rest of the floor (after adding proper structural reinforcement) to open it up to the downstairs living space.

In an attic with little headroom, remove the entire floor so that the room below is open all the way to the roof. Then add a loft and use it as a retreat, a bedroom, or storage space.

For a retreat, consider:
☐ Comfortable seating that could also be used for sleeping
☐ At least one window or skylight
☐ Mirrors on the sloped ceiling to enlarge the space

Apartments

If you have an area that measures at least 400 square feet, you might be able to create an apartment to generate rental income.

Local zoning and building regulations vary. Sometimes apartments are not allowed; therefore, check with your building department before installing one. Even if an apartment is legal, there are often stipulations. These may pertain to minimum allowable lot size, maximum floor area, maximum number of bedrooms, separate utility meters, respect for neighbors' privacy, maximum number of occupants, adequate off-street parking, and special fire precautions.

Soft gray walls are punctuated by a white-framed window and geometric-patterned wallcovering. Small-scale fabrics and furnishings are generally more appropriate in a low-roofed attic. Here an open-arm side chair provides a comfortable spot to enjoy a book, without overpowering the space.

DEFINING THE SPACE

The goal of attic design is to plan a space that meets all your practical needs in a pleasing, affordable way. This can be achieved by a creative process that begins when you have identified your needs and priorities and ends when a set of construction documents is complete.

After considering possible uses for your attic, you probably have a pretty good idea—perhaps even a complete picture—of what sort of room is desired. Design is the process of creating plans that come as close to that picture as possible.

In developing a design, whether working alone or with a professional, you must first define the space. Assess your attic and adapt the space to meet your functional needs. Then refine the design, adding finish details and other features that will give the space overall character.

The following pages describe issues that will affect your design. Whether you are planning the new space yourself or with a designer, these issues, which can affect one another, will have to be addressed, regardless of the size of the project.

In developing your design, consider structure and use factors first. These will shape the space you have to work with and determine the possibilities for basic comfort and practicality. Knowing what structural work will be required gives you an early indication of whether your plans will fit your budget. If not, you will have to decide which to change—your budget or your plans.

As you assess the attic space and consider changes, use a floor plan, a note pad, or rough sketches to keep track of your thoughts.

Is there enough space?
One of the first questions to ask is whether your attic is large enough to be converted. At some point, you will need to make accurate calculations, but you can quickly measure the floor area and ceiling height to obtain ballpark figures.

Floor area
Codes specify the minimum size of a room intended for certain uses. The chart that follows summarizes minimum floor areas specified by HUD and many local codes. (Be sure to check your local building code.) The sample includes a minimum room size and a preferred size that would make it much more comfortable. As the minimum sizes are quite small, design larger rooms when possible. If figures are omitted, there is usually no minimum code requirement.

Ceiling height
In addition to minimum floor area, there is also a requirement for minimum ceiling height: generally 7½ feet. Bathrooms, hallways, and kitchens are an exception; in these rooms the minimum is usually 7 feet. Rooms with sloped ceilings, such as attics, are also exceptions: Only 50 percent of the ceiling over the required floor area needs to be 7½ feet or higher. However, floor space with less than 5 feet of ceiling height cannot be included in the final computation of allowable floor area.

If your attic is unfinished, you can determine if there is enough ceiling height by measuring the distance between the attic floor and the bottom of the roof rafters at the ridge. As a rule of thumb, this dimension should be at least 9 feet. It should be more if you are increasing the size of floor joists or roof rafters.

Room sizes

Room	Minimum floor area*	Sample size	Preferred size
Bedroom	80 sq ft	8' by 10'	11' by 14'
Master bedroom	—	—	12' by 16'
Family room	110 sq ft	10.5' by 10.5'	12' by 16'
Living room	176 sq ft	11' by 16'	12' by 18'
Other habitable room	70 sq ft	7' by 10'	—
Bathroom	35 sq ft	5' by 7'	5' by 9'
Toilet compartment	—	min. 30" wide	—
Apartment	min. 400 sq ft	—	—

*Means net floor area within enclosing walls, excluding built-in fixtures, closets, or cabinets

Size requirements

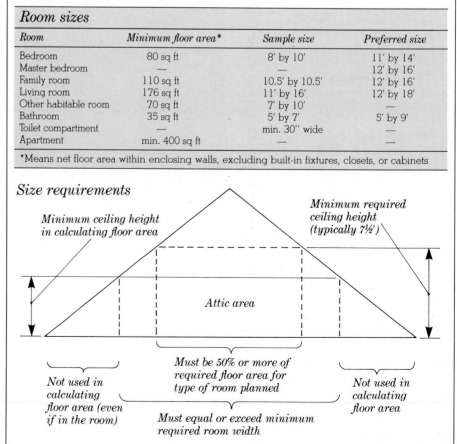

Minimum ceiling height in calculating floor area

Minimum required ceiling height (typically 7½')

Attic area

Not used in calculating floor area (even if in the room)

Must be 50% or more of required floor area for type of room planned

Not used in calculating floor area

Must equal or exceed minimum required room width

Is there enough headroom?

If there is not enough space to turn your attic into the room you are planning, there are ways to enlarge it. These measures increase the amount of usable floor area by creating more headroom. Some of them are fairly simple; others involve complex structural changes that can be very costly. Read the following text and study the illustrations to determine whether it is possible to gain headroom.

If none of the measures described here give you the space you need, consider converting the attic into storage space or a sleeping loft. Then you might be able to rearrange downstairs rooms to gain needed additional living space.

A word of caution: No structural changes should be considered without the advice of a competent architect or engineer.

Gaining height

Collar ties, or rafter ties, are the horizontal boards nailed between pairs of rafters. The ties keep the rafters from spreading apart or sagging. Because they are often below the required ceiling height for living space, it is very tempting to remove them to get them out of the way. However, they are vital supports for the roof, which could be seriously weakened by their removal.

Raising collar ties. Sometimes the ties are only 4 to 6 inches too low for adequate headroom. In that case, you can simply raise them.

Removing collar ties. You may be able to remove some of the collar ties as long as the remaining ones are at least 80 inches from the floor and spaced no more than 4 feet apart.

If removing all the collar ties is the only way to get headroom, the rafters must be tied together with the old ceiling joists or new floor joists. The rafters may also need intermediate support. This is usually provided by kneewalls (low walls corresponding to the pitch of the roof) or beams. If you want an entirely open space with no kneewalls or beams, reinforce the rafters with new rafters.

Raising or removing ceiling joists. If you have a finished attic with a low ceiling, you may be able to raise it or remove it without disturbing the roof. Treat the ceiling joists like collar ties, unless you are certain that they support only the ceiling and are not part of the roof structure.

Caution. The one type of roof structure that cannot be altered is a truss system. Trusses are carefully engineered and cannot sustain extra loads on the bottom chord (the attic floor). Nor can any members be cut without danger of collapse.

Roof trusses are common in newer homes, especially tract developments and are characterized by a cluster of supporting members. This type of roof framing usually makes an attic conversion impossible.

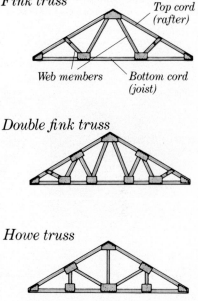

Fink truss

Top cord (rafter)

Web members   Bottom cord (joist)

Double fink truss

Howe truss

Lowering the floor

If your downstairs rooms have high ceilings, you may be able to lower the attic floor enough to provide the required attic headroom. Even with conventional ceiling heights, you may be able to drop the ceiling in some areas where it will not affect living space: over closets or a garage, for example. This technique is particularly suitable for a small attic room that will be used as a den, sleeping loft, or quiet retreat.

Lowering the attic floor is a radical change because it destroys the triangular structure of the roof system. Extra headers, new beams, tie rods, or similar devices can be installed for reinforcement, however.

Roof framing

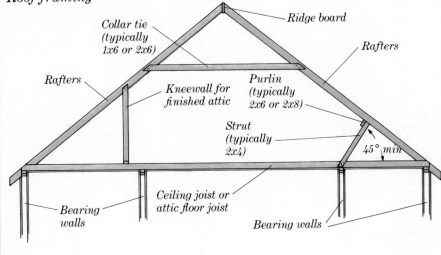

Collar tie (typically 1x6 or 2x6)

Ridge board

Rafters

Rafters

Kneewall for finished attic

Purlin (typically 2x6 or 2x8)

Strut (typically 2x4)

45° min

Bearing walls

Ceiling joist or attic floor joist

Bearing walls

Adding a dormer

A dormer increases headroom over a small amount of floor area and makes new windows possible. The two basic dormer shapes are gable and shed.

Gable. A gable dormer has charm and appeal, reflecting the basic lines of most houses. It cannot be very large, so it adds light but little floor space. You often need more than one gable dormer to provide a balanced look to the exterior of the house.

Shed. A shed dormer adds more living space than a gable dormer. It can even extend across the entire length of the roof, although this option may be appropriate only if the dormer faces the backyard.

Raising the roof

Raising a roof usually requires rebuilding large portions, if not all, of it. The most efficient strategy is to leave half of a gable roof intact and raise the other half, like a large shed dormer. The ridge must be supported by a new beam.

Another possibility is to rebuild the roof at a much steeper pitch. Both projects are expensive but may be practical if the roof needs replacing.

Even if your present attic has a floor, the joists may be sized only for light loads such as storage, not the heavier loads imposed by normal living. If so, they will need to be reinforced.

To determine whether the existing joists are adequate for an attic conversion, follow these steps.

☐ Measure the span of each of the existing joists.

☐ Measure the spacing between the joists (12, 16, or 24 inches on center).

☐ Check the joist span opposite to see what size joists are required for that span and spacing. If your joists are the size indicated or larger, they are probably adequate and you can lay a subfloor directly over them. You should, however, get professional advice before proceeding because the joist requirements in the chart are minimums and depend on the grade and species of lumber used. There may also be areas of the floor that require an extra joist or two because of concentrated loads, such as a large bathtub, a bearing wall, or a stairwell.

Are the walls adequate?

Converting an attic into living space is like adding an extra story to your home. You may need to reinforce the foundation or the walls unless the house was originally built to support an extra floor.

Foundation walls

A foundation built for a one-story home is typically 6 inches wide on top and 12 inches wide at the footing. There are several ways to strengthen it for an additional story. In all cases you will need the advice and expertise of an architect, engineer, or building contractor.

Expand the foundation footing. You can expand the footing by pouring a grade beam next to it. Tie the two masses of concrete together with

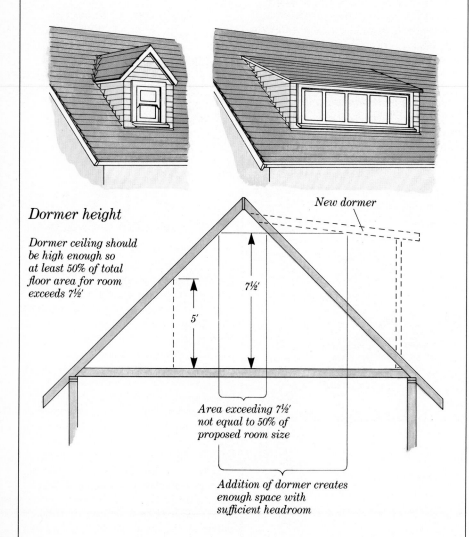

Gabled dormer

Shed dormer

Dormer height

Dormer ceiling should be high enough so at least 50% of total floor area for room exceeds 7½'

7½'

5'

New dormer

Area exceeding 7½' not equal to 50% of proposed room size

Addition of dormer creates enough space with sufficient headroom

dowels set into the original footing before the new beam is poured.

Pour concrete pads. Another method is to pour new concrete pads beneath the existing foundation at strategic points where loads from the attic will be concentrated.

Rebuild the foundation. You may need to remove the existing foundation, especially if it is weak or crumbling, and build a new foundation designed for the extra story.

Cripple walls or kneewalls

If the house is already two stories high, the short wall between the foundation and first floor may need to be reinforced to support new attic living space. This wall is sometimes called a cripple wall or kneewall and must have 2 by 6 studs, 16 inches on center, to support three stories. If the existing studs are 2 by 4s, double them up or replace them with new 2 by 6 studs.

First-floor walls may also need reinforcement. An attic living space can increase lateral forces on the house in an earthquake or high winds. Local building codes may require you to counteract these forces by adding shear strength to the downstairs bearing walls. In most cases such strengthening involves stripping away siding or the interior finish wall and then nailing plywood panels directly to the wall framing. This may be required along the entire length of the bearing wall, or only at corners and other vital points.

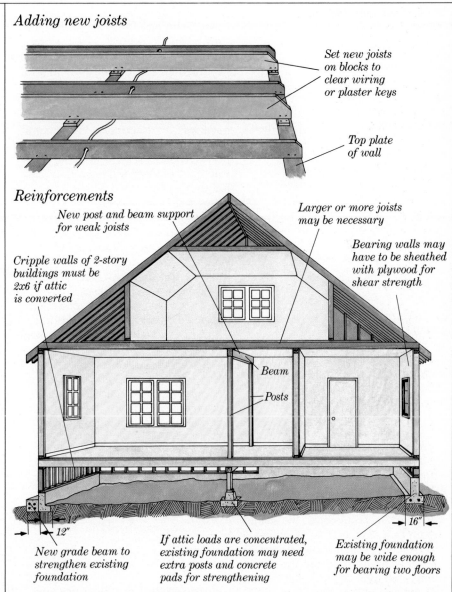

Adding new joists

Set new joists on blocks to clear wiring or plaster keys

Top plate of wall

Reinforcements

New post and beam support for weak joists

Larger or more joists may be necessary

Cripple walls of 2-story buildings must be 2x6 if attic is converted

Bearing walls may have to be sheathed with plywood for shear strength

Beam

Posts

12"

New grade beam to strengthen existing foundation

If attic loads are concentrated, existing foundation may need extra posts and concrete pads for strengthening

16"

Existing foundation may be wide enough for bearing two floors

Floor joists

Allowable spans for 40 pounds per square foot live load. Listed in feet and inches. The figures labeled o.c. mean inches on center.

Joist size	Joist spacing	Modules of elasticity, E, in 1,000,000 psi													
		0.8	0.9	1.0	1.1	1.2	1.3	1.4	1.5	1.6	1.7	1.8	1.9	2.0	2.2
2x6	16 o.c.	7-9	8-0	8-4	8-4	8-10	9-1	9-4	9-6	9-9	9-11	10-2	10-4	10-6	10-10
	24 o.c.	6-9	7-0	7-3	7-6	7-9	7-11	8-2	8-4	8-6	8-8	8-10	9-0	9-2	9-6
2x8	16 o.c.	10-2	10-7	11-0	11-4	11-8	12-0	12-3	12-7	12-10	13-1	13-4	13-7	13-10	14-3
	24 o.c.	8-11	9-3	9-7	9-11	10-2	10-6	10-9	11-0	11-3	11-5	11-8	11-11	12-1	12-6
2x10	16 o.c.	13-0	13-6	14-0	14-6	14-11	15-3	15-8	16-0	16-5	16-9	17-0	17-4	17-8	18-3
	24 o.c.	11-4	11-10	12-3	12-8	13-0	13-4	13-8	14-0	14-4	14-7	14-11	15-2	15-5	15-11
2x12	16 o.c.	15-10	16-5	17-0	17-7	18-1	18-7	19-1	19-6	19-11	20-4	20-9	21-1	21-6	22-2
	24 o.c.	13-10	14-4	14-11	15-4	15-10	16-3	16-8	17-0	17-5	17-9	18-1	18-5	18-9	19-4

Is there adequate access?

An attic needs stairs. If you already have a comfortable and safe stairway, there is no problem. However, many attic stairs are intended for limited use and will not qualify as a primary stairway: They may be too steep or too narrow.

Minimum stair requirements

The minimum requirements for most primary stairways are:
7½-inch maximum riser height
9-inch minimum tread width
30 inches between handrails

Local codes may vary, and you will need to find out if your stairway must be altered to meet your code.

Locating stairs

Even if the stairway meets minimum code requirements, look carefully at both the location and the style of the stairs. Consider stair placement in terms of the attic space and the downstairs rooms, keeping the following factors in mind.

Headroom. Attic stairs are usually located under or close to the roof ridge because the area near the eaves rarely has enough headroom.

Convenience. If you are building several rooms in the attic, the stairs should be convenient to all of them. They should be positioned so that it is not necessary to pass through a bedroom or a bathroom to reach them.

If the attic will be used for family gatherings, the stairs should be convenient to the rest of the house, particularly the kitchen. If there are to be bedrooms in the attic, consider privacy factors and the convenience of laundry facilities.

Noise. Because noise travels up and down stairs easily, stairs should not connect quiet and noisy rooms. If there is no alternative, consider an insulated stairwell and weather stripping on the doors to reduce sound transmission.

Emergency egress. Sleeping space in the attic must have an emergency exit as well as main stairs. This is usually an openable window. If you are planning a small deck, balcony, or separate apartment, you may want to build an exterior stairway in addition to the main stairs.

Structural support. If you need to cut a hole in the floor for a new stairway, try to position the stairwell so it runs parallel to the floor joists. If it runs perpendicular to them, a great number of joists will have to be cut and then supported with a beam or a new wall downstairs.

Aesthetics. Try to arrange for an appealing view when ascending and descending. A window, an attractive room, or a charming alcove will be more appealing than a stark wall or drab hallway. The strategic placement of a skylight in the attic ceiling above the stairwell will also bring daylight and a sense of space to some of the rooms downstairs.

If you can take the space from large downstairs rooms, consider enlarging a narrow stairwell to make it more appealing. Use the space under and around the stairs for storage.

Stair terminology

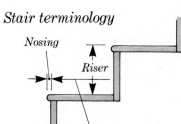

Nosing

Riser

Tread

Saving space

If the space does not exist, it may not be possible to create the perfect stairway. Stairways take up a lot more room than most people realize. A simple straight-run stairway from one floor to the next requires almost 50 square feet of floor area downstairs and 35 to 40 square feet of floor area upstairs for the well. This is almost like adding another room to the house. Other configurations, such as L-shaped or U-shaped stairways, take up even more space.

Steeper stairs. Making stairs steeper will shorten them, but it is safe only if riser height and tread width meet minimum requirements.

Spiral stairs. Prefabricated spiral stairways take up much less floor space than conventional stairs. Their diameters vary from 4 to 6 feet. Most codes specify that a spiral stairway cannot be used as a primary stairway if the total upper floor area is larger than 400 square feet. Also, it is hard to move furniture up and down spiral stairs. They are an excellent solution for small lofts and retreats, however, and work well as secondary stairways.

Winders. Stairs that wind around a sharp turn save space by eliminating the need for a landing, but they can be dangerous if not built properly. Strict codes regulate the size, and they are not permitted in some areas.

Sample stairway dimensions

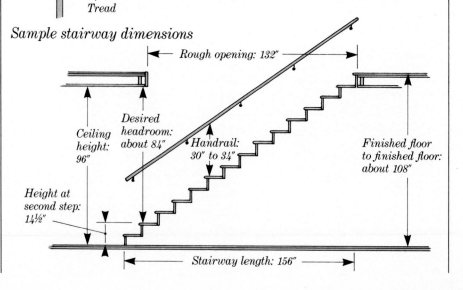

Rough opening: 132"

Ceiling height: 96"

Desired headroom: about 84"

Handrail: 30" to 34"

Finished floor to finished floor: about 108"

Height at second step: 14½"

Stairway length: 156"

Are there obstructions?

It is rare to find an unfinished attic that is not cluttered with pipes, flues, vents, chimneys, framing members, and other essential but annoying obstacles. Some can be moved or removed altogether. Obstacles that cannot be moved must be incorporated into walls or storage units or be left exposed.

Moving and removing obstructions

As you plan the placement of walls and the arrangement of rooms in your attic, consider these possibilities for dealing with obstructions.

Plumbing vents. These can usually be moved or incorporated into the plumbing for new attic fixtures if they are 1½- or 2-inch diameter pipes. A 3- or 4-inch main stack is harder to move, but not impossible.

Heating ducts. If they create impassable barriers on the attic floor, heating ducts must be moved. It is usually possible to move them into the empty eave space located behind the attic kneewalls.

Flues. Flues for downstairs stoves and appliances can usually be rerouted. Flues for obsolete trash burners or furnaces that have been replaced can be totally removed.

Sometimes you can change the location of the flue in a downstairs room so it runs straight up through the attic without interfering with attic living space. To do this, you must maintain required clearances from walls and ceiling, make sure that the ratio of horizontal length to total vertical length will not exceed the allowable maximum (usually 75 percent), and check that the horizontal run will have the pitch and angled fittings required by local mechanical code.

You may also be able to vent a downstairs appliance out a side wall, bypassing the attic and roof. Some codes allow this as long as the vent terminates in a special wall thimble. Usually such vents are allowed only on appliances with sealed combustion units, and they must be on a wall in the same room as the appliance. Check local codes carefully.

Working around immovable obstructions

If the obstruction is a chimney, major flue, large plumbing vent, or posts supporting ridge beams, there are two options. Either leave the obstruction exposed, or conceal it by boxing it in or incorporating it into a wall.

Expose. As long as the bricks are reasonably attractive, a brick chimney can actually be a design asset.

If concealing a pipe or duct seems too awkward, try a high-tech design approach: Paint it a bright color and leave it exposed.

Conceal. If the obstacle lacks design appeal, it can be boxed in with simple framing and wallboard. This approach works best if you include a shelving unit, a closet, a built-in table, or a seating platform as part of the boxing unit.

In some cases, box framing can be built around the obstruction in the form of a decorative column.

Working around obstructions

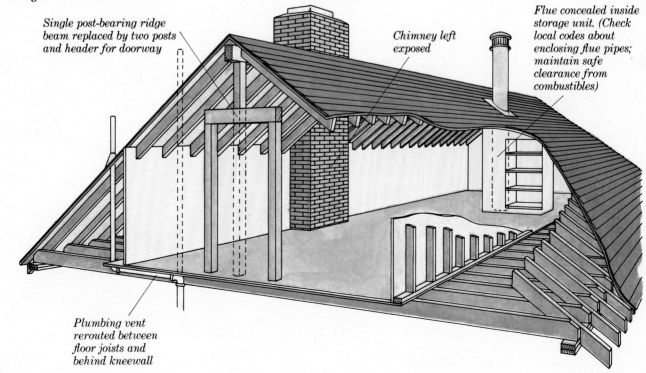

Single post-bearing ridge beam replaced by two posts and header for doorway

Chimney left exposed

Flue concealed inside storage unit. (Check local codes about enclosing flue pipes; maintain safe clearance from combustibles)

Plumbing vent rerouted between floor joists and behind kneewall

Is there enough daylight?

Many attics have only a single shaft of light streaming through a small window in the end wall, but this does not mean you have to settle for only one or two gable windows. You can open up the attic to natural daylight with skylights and roof windows as well as with conventional windows placed in gable walls or dormers. Skylights and overhead windows admit up to five times as much light as do conventional windows. The following suggestions will help you select and place windows and skylights.

Balancing the light. Natural light should come from more than one direction to make a room comfortable. To avoid unbalanced light, place windows on different walls, use a window and a skylight, or use two roof windows on opposite slopes of the roof.

Overheating. To prevent overheating, especially from skylights or roof windows, most skylight manufacturers offer shading devices. They also offer opaque and bronzed glazing, and openable units to let hot air out. To prevent overheating, locate skylights on north-facing slopes of the roof or place them where trees will provide shade.

Heat loss. To prevent heat loss, use insulating windows and skylights. You can also install removable insulation devices that cover windows on cold winter nights.

Views. As a rule, it is not comfortable to look out of a window so low that the horizon cannot be seen. Windows at eye level are fine, and windows placed too high to see the horizon are quite comfortable and even inspiring. Consider both your own privacy and your neighbors'. A high window solves both problems. Trees, balconies, and high fences will also help.

Safety. Avoid low windows that toddlers may run into. Use tempered glass or other approved glazing for skylights.

Placement. Make sure that windows will not be blocked by tall furniture. Place a window where there will be an informal reading or conversation area. If you enjoy sleeping under the stars, locate a skylight directly over your bed.

Exterior architecture. Although a pleasing interior should be your first concern, it is important to consider how new windows will affect the exterior look of your home. This is especially true if the house is an architectural treasure or if there are strict neighborhood codes governing all exterior changes.

Letting in light

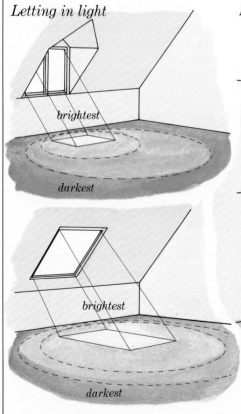

A roof window or skylight lets in up to five times more light than a conventional window and is less likely to be obstructed by trees or buildings

Balancing light

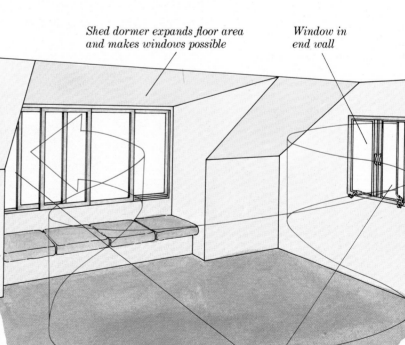

Shed dormer expands floor area and makes windows possible

Window in end wall

Open windows allow for cross ventilation

Is there enough ventilation?

Attics need fresh air. The typical code requirement for a window-opening area is at least one twentieth of the floor area in a room and no less than 5 square feet.

Ventilating skylight. A single ventilating skylight exhausts warm, stale air, which is usually replaced by similar air from the rest of the house. However, it may admit some fresh air if you place it low on the roof slope or if it is a pivot window that opens at both top and bottom.

Cross-ventilation. More effective ventilation is achieved by placing openable windows or skylights opposite each other, creating a cross-breeze. Position them carefully so that you will gain maximum benefit from the prevailing winds.

Air-conditioning. Ventilation from mechanical systems may be unnecessary if windows and skylights provide the required temperatures. If you do choose to install a mechanical system, it must provide at least one fresh-air exchange per hour to give proper ventilation.

A large window makes a small attic bedroom appear much more spacious and, because privacy generally is not a problem, it can be left uncovered. Bunk beds free a generous amount of floor area for a child's daytime activities.

Is the wiring adequate?

Any new living space requires additional wiring. It may be necessary to upgrade the house system to accommodate new attic wiring, but the arrangement of the actual attic space will not be affected by wiring requirements. New wiring can be planned around a space and need only meet safety and convenience needs. You can plan the wiring after the final design is complete.

The following are some guidelines for attic circuits and fixtures.

☐ Provide at least one general purpose circuit for lighting.

☐ Place a switch that controls a light or an outlet close to each entrance in every room.

☐ Place at least one outlet on each wall over 2 feet long. (No point along any wall should be more than 6 feet from an outlet.)

☐ Provide additional outlets or junction boxes for any fixed appliances such as heaters, disposers, or laundry equipment.

☐ Make sure stairways and halls are well lit. Place switches at both ends.

New circuits. It may be possible to wire the attic by extending existing circuits, but it is better to run completely new circuits. If there will be more than two or three circuits, plan on installing a subpanel in the attic rather than running wires for each new circuit all the way down to the main service panel. The existing panel may not even have room for new breakers.

Work spaces and media rooms. These areas need more outlets than a conventional room and may also require low-voltage speaker wiring, computer cables, and telephone cables. You may need professional help to do this type of wiring.

Smoke alarms. It is a good idea to wire smoke alarms into the house wiring rather than relying on battery-operated smoke alarms for attic rooms. If the room is a bedroom, codes may demand this.

Relocating wiring. If you are installing new floor joists, you may have to move wiring for some of the downstairs rooms. In most cases it is a simple matter to remove the old wiring and run new wires after the floor joists are installed.

Outdoor lighting. While you are planning attic wiring, consider outdoor lighting. If you would like floodlights or other outdoor lights mounted high on the house exterior, install these when wiring the attic.

Wiring

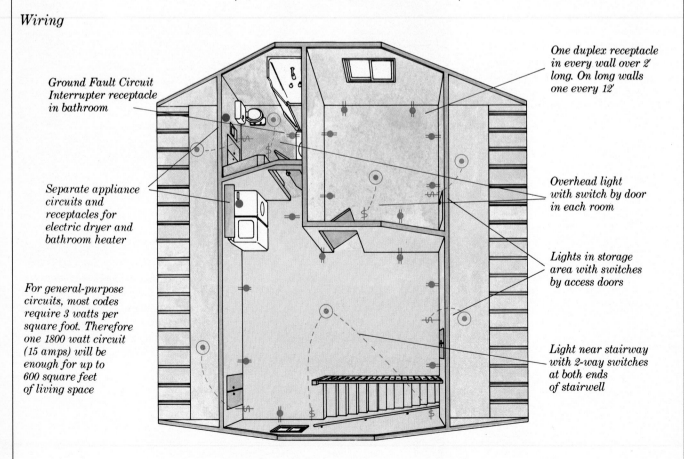

Ground Fault Circuit Interrupter receptacle in bathroom

Separate appliance circuits and receptacles for electric dryer and bathroom heater

For general-purpose circuits, most codes require 3 watts per square foot. Therefore one 1800 watt circuit (15 amps) will be enough for up to 600 square feet of living space

One duplex receptacle in every wall over 2' long. On long walls one every 12'

Overhead light with switch by door in each room

Lights in storage area with switches by access doors

Light near stairway with 2-way switches at both ends of stairwell

Are plumbing hookups possible?

The two main concerns regarding plumbing are planning the location of new fixtures and moving any existing plumbing that is in the way.

Location. Locate new fixtures for a bathroom, laundry, or wet bar where they will be easiest to hook up. Drainpipes are the most critical because they have to be precisely aligned to work properly and because they intrude into the downstairs space. Vents and water-supply pipes are not as big a problem.

The ideal location for fixtures is above a downstairs bathroom with a soil stack that can be used as a drain (if your local plumbing code allows this). The next best option is to place fixtures where the drainpipe can run through a downstairs closet or utility room. (Conceal the pipe simply by boxing it in.)

If neither of these options will work, you can locate fixtures over the middle of downstairs rooms by running the drain horizontally before it turns downward into a closet or other concealed space. If the drain runs parallel to the attic floor joists and the joists are large enough to accommodate the diameter and slope of the drainpipe, you can conceal the pipe between them.

If the joists are too small or the drain cannot be run parallel to them, the pipe must be positioned below the joists. This makes it intrude into the ceiling space of the room below, requiring a soffit or other box to conceal it. If this is unacceptable, build a raised floor in the attic and hide the drainipe inside it. Be sure there is enough headroom.

Hidden plumbing. Access to hidden plumbing may also affect fixture location. A tub faucet must have a door or removable panel behind it for access. All cleanouts (usually located at the upstream end of horizontal runs) must be accessible. This may require installing an access panel in the downstairs ceiling, preferably in a closet, hallway, or utility room.

Existing vents. An existing plumbing vent can be moved fairly easily. Cut it off below the floor level, change direction with a quarter-turn fitting, run a horizontal pipe between the floor joists to a point behind the kneewall, and change its direction back to a vertical pipe.

Vent pipes can be concealed in partition or gable walls. They can also be connected to other vents as long as the size is not reduced. (The total cross-sectional area of all vents must equal or exceed the cross-sectional area of the main drain.) Just be sure that no vents terminate inside the attic space. All vents must extend up through the roof and terminate at least 12 inches above it.

New fixtures. When shopping for new fixtures, consider their weight, height, and size. A luxury bathtub filled with water and two bathers can weigh as much as 1,500 pounds.

Shower stalls require a ceiling height of 7 feet or more, or an average of 6 feet, 10 inches for sloped ceilings. Sometimes the only possible location for a shower is directly under the roof ridge. If a sink or toilet is to be placed under a sloped ceiling, be sure there is enough headroom to stand comfortably. If you are considering any large fixtures, such as a luxury bathtub or a one-piece tub/shower unit, be sure you can get them up the stairs.

If you are planning to install a gas heater or stove, consult with a plumbing or heating specialist to be sure the present gas lines are the correct size to accommodate an appliance.

Plumbing

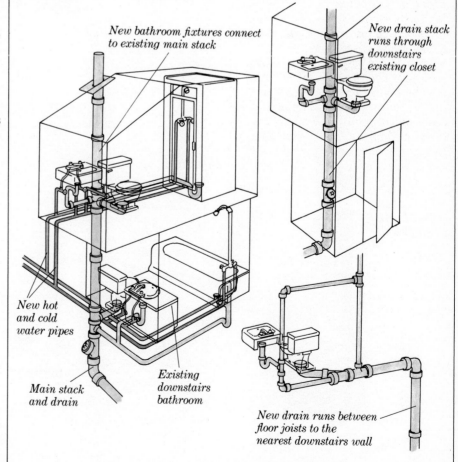

New bathroom fixtures connect to existing main stack

New drain stack runs through downstairs existing closet

New hot and cold water pipes

Main stack and drain

Existing downstairs bathroom

New drain runs between floor joists to the nearest downstairs wall

Can the space be heated and cooled?

The usual way to heat attics is with electric baseboard heaters or small gas heaters. Because attics collect heat from the rest of the house, you probably will not turn on these heaters very often.

Central heating

If your home has a central forced-air or hydronic (hot water or steam) heating system, it may be a simple matter to heat the attic by extending the ductwork, which may have to be moved out of the way in order to create living space. You can relocate the ducts behind the attic kneewalls or enclose them in a thick wall down the center of the attic (as long as they will not interrupt any doorways).

Stove or fireplace

Proximity to the roof makes it easier to install a chimney in the attic than in a downstairs room. However, you must allow for the weight when planning your floor framing system. Also think about the inconvenience of having to carry firewood up and ashes down when you use either a stove or fireplace. Check your local code for installation requirements.

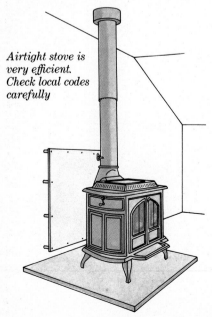

Airtight stove is very efficient. Check local codes carefully

Heat Circulation

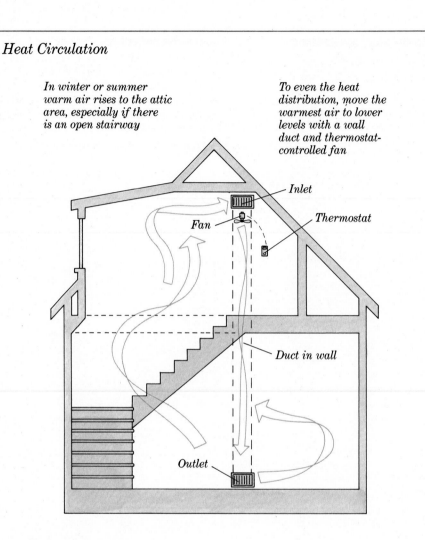

In winter or summer warm air rises to the attic area, especially if there is an open stairway

To even the heat distribution, move the warmest air to lower levels with a wall duct and thermostat-controlled fan

Inlet

Fan

Thermostat

Duct in wall

Outlet

Central heat

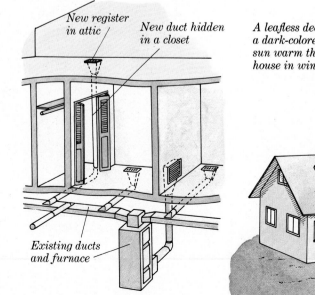

New register in attic

New duct hidden in a closet

Existing ducts and furnace

A leafless deciduous tree and a dark-colored roof let the sun warm the attic and house in winter

Cooling

Cooling an attic is very important. It affects both the actual space and the rooms downstairs. Use as many natural cooling methods in your design as possible. Include cross-ventilation from openable windows and skylights, light-colored roofing materials, overhead shade from trees, and ventilation in adjacent spaces, such as enclosed eaves or hidden areas above the ceiling.

If natural cooling methods are not enough, consider a large paddle fan on the attic ceiling. Or install either an independent room air conditioner or an extension of the existing central air-conditioning system.

The leafy tree shades the house to keep it cooler in summer

Paddle fans help cooling and heating by circulating the air

Should the space be insulated?

As living space, your attic will need a blanket of insulation all around it. Local building codes will specify the amount required in your area.

Most codes require a ventilated air space above any ceiling insulation. To make room for thick roof insulation plus the required air space, you will probably have to nail 2 by 2 furring strips below, or even install new 2 by 12 rafters next to, the old rafters. If the roof is weak or if you want to remove collar ties, purlins, or kneewalls, you may have to install the larger rafters anyway.

If fiberglass blanket insulation is too thick, use rigid foam or fiberglass boards. Foam boards are flammable and must be covered with wallboard for fireproofing. Rigid fiberglass can be exposed directly to the living space. These panels are convenient

to use when you want the rafters to show as exposed ceiling beams or if you cannot increase the rafter size because of limited headroom.

Insulation is not needed in the attic floor over heated living space. If it is there already, leave it there to help with sound insulation and to prevent excessive heat loss from downstairs.

Sound insulation

Consider these ways to prevent noise from traveling through the attic floor.
☐ Install carpeting with a thick pad.
☐ Place sound-deadening panels over the joists and under the subfloor.
☐ Install a "floating floor"—fiberglass blankets installed directly over the attic subfloor with another subfloor laid over them.
☐ Fasten the downstairs ceiling wallboard to resilient metal channels rather than to the attic floor joists.
☐ Apply weather stripping around the stairwell door.

Insulation

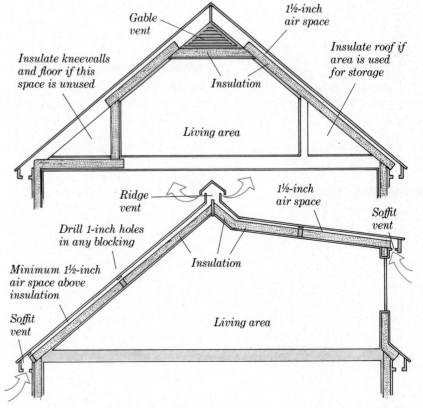

Gable vent

1½-inch air space

Insulate kneewalls and floor if this space is unused

Insulation

Insulate roof if area is used for storage

Living area

Ridge vent

1½-inch air space

Soffit vent

Drill 1-inch holes in any blocking

Insulation

Minimum 1½-inch air space above insulation

Soffit vent

Living area

REFINING YOUR DESIGN

Refining the space gives you only a basic idea of what it will look like and how you can take care of practical necessities. The next step is to refine a design until the entire space feels integrated and complete.

Refining a design means finding a balance between the available space, the intended uses, and the desired effect. It includes:

☐ Making a priority list of the desires for your home
☐ Listing the activities and needs for each room
☐ Adopting special strategies where space is limited
☐ Planning storage
☐ Choosing finish materials
☐ Adding features that give your attic a special appeal

You will need to put a great deal of work into this process, whether you are working with a professional or not. There are many alternatives to consider and decisions to make, but after several refinements a design will emerge that works. A completed design will make the best use of available space for the activities you plan, and it will create a space that delights in a special way.

Can you enlarge without altering?

If your attic is cramped, you can enlarge the space without altering the structure at all. You can make space feel and even live bigger by employing some of the following strategies.

☐ Use areas with the highest headroom for traffic and circulation, not furniture placement.
☐ Locate chairs, sofas, beds, and desks close to the eaves, where it is too low to walk or stand.
☐ Make maximum use of built-ins, especially hidden storage under the eaves and in walls between rooms.
☐ Use multipurpose furnishings, such as a seating platform that also functions as a bed, a drop-leaf end table that can be used as a dining table, a wicker hamper that doubles as an end table, a bookcase that has a tilt-down desk top.
☐ Use furnishings of an appropriate scale such as low-back chairs, which do not dominate a space as much as high-back ones.
☐ Cluster furnishings in groups to increase their usefulness and create wider traffic corridors.
☐ Consider dividers instead of full-height walls to create separate areas.
☐ Use a light, neutral-colored wall-to-wall floor covering.
☐ Use light colors for wallcoverings and other large, flat surfaces.
☐ Use strong horizontal lines to make a room feel longer.
☐ Accentuate vertical lines to make the ceiling feel higher.
☐ Locate windows in the corner instead of the center of a wall.

Is there enough storage?

Efficient, well-designed storage is an important element in any design, but attics offer more opportunities for hidden or built-in storage than do more conventionally shaped rooms.

Making the best use of space

Storage strategies that work in other rooms in the house will also work well in attics. Closets can be organized with dividers and shelf units for maximum efficiency. Platform beds can have built-in storage units underneath. The spaces above doorways and around fireplaces are potential locations for shelves and storage units, as are any other nooks and crannies that you can find.

Instead of armchairs, use built-in benches with storage underneath.

Instead of a table pushed against a wall, use a storage unit with a fold-down table top. Instead of taking up floor space with a dresser, build the unit into a kneewall with the drawer faces flush with the wall surface.

Built-ins

Custom-built storage units are often necessary because of the unique angles and nonstandard wall heights found in an attic.

Behind kneewalls. Usually there is abundant space for hidden storage behind kneewalls, although it is difficult to get to. For easier access, use the kneewalls for recessed shelves or cubbyholes. This limits the placement of furniture unless you omit shelves along part of the wall.

Shelves can also be built in front of the kneewall. A long row of low shelves will help to make a small room feel larger.

Under eaves. If the attic room has no kneewalls (if the floor extends all the way to the back of the eaves), the open eaves can be used for built-in storage units such as cabinets, drawer units, or low closets.

This space can also be used for open storage if you have large, attractive objects to store. They will be out of the way and easily accessible.

Around the stairwell. Another place for built-in storage is around the stairwell. Instead of an open bannister, enclose the stairwell with a low, solid wall for the railing. Build shelves or cubbyholes into it for storing and displaying attractive objects.

Using wall space

Custom units are not the only option for attic spaces. Modular units also work well. They are compact and efficient, and the uniform height and clean lines are more appropriate for a small space than is assorted shelving at random heights. Just be sure that the strong, rectilinear shape of such units fits into all the odd angles and spaces formed by attic walls.

Shelves and cabinets can be incorporated into partition walls between attic rooms. Exterior walls cannot have cubbyholes built into them because they are filled with insulation, but you can build or buy shelving units that attach to the walls.

A gable wall is an excellent place to build wall-to-ceiling shelving. On an end wall that has a window in it, shelving can frame the window, extending across the top and on either side. You could even include a small window seat below the window.

Concealed storage

If you do not need all of the attic for living space, you can leave some of it unfinished and use it for a storage room, especially if you have furniture and other large objects to store.

Above the ceiling. The attic ceiling is another potential storage area. If you are planning a level ceiling, there will be a hidden space under the roof ridge that is large enough for storage. For access, make a scuttle (hatch) in the ceiling or dividing wall.

Even if you do not install a level ceiling in the attic, you can build small storage platforms below the roof ridge. These should be at least 7 feet above the finish floor and will look best positioned at the ends of the room rather than over the center portion of the space.

Storage

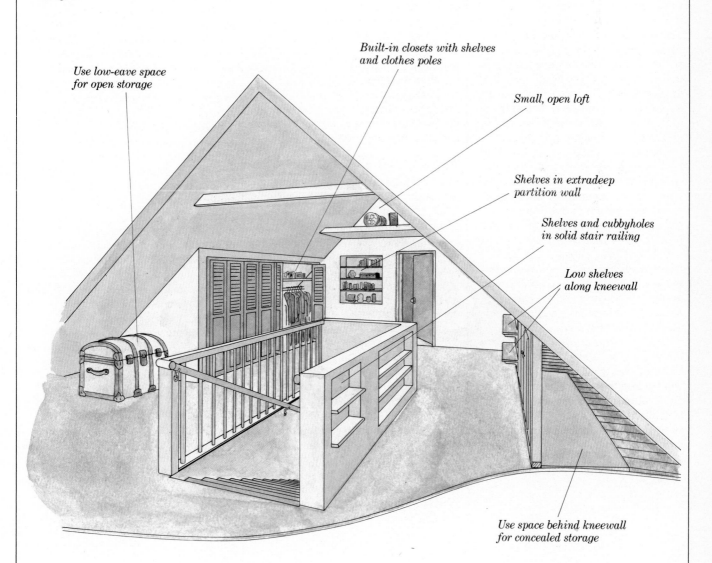

Use low-eave space for open storage

Built-in closets with shelves and clothes poles

Small, open loft

Shelves in extradeep partition wall

Shelves and cubbyholes in solid stair railing

Low shelves along kneewall

Use space behind kneewall for concealed storage

What finish details can be used?

Your final design will include specifications for wall surfaces, floor coverings, trim materials, doors, light fixtures, hardware, plumbing fixtures, and other finish details. All of these elements have a strong impact on the space because they become the textures, shapes, and colors that you live with. You will play a major role in choosing them.

It is easy to put off these decisions until you see the actual space, and many people do. Often the architect simply specifies "furnished by owner" for some of the details in the plans, and an allowance is included in the contractor's bid package. This approach is valid, but you should try to decide on all these details during the design phase, even if you end up making changes later on.

One reason for planning finish details early is that these features represent a significant part of the budget. Considering them at the outset minimizes the chance of overlooking an expensive item and gives you time to research all available options.

Some of your choices may also affect other design issues. When the plans are still being formed and your architect and designer are thinking about the details, take advantage of their professional advice.

Finally, if you know that every detail of the plan is settled before the bidding and construction begin, you will be free to focus on problems and issues at hand. You can even anticipate them rather than having the project languish because an important decision has not been made or a key item is not procured.

What are the design choices?

Your choices will vary according to functional needs, cost, overall feeling of the space, and individual preference. Except for the following considerations, choosing materials for an attic is the same as choosing them for any other room.

Floor coverings

If you want the space to feel larger, use a continuous floor covering of one color rather than scatter rugs or a highly patterned material.

Carpet muffles sound and gives a more inviting feel to low areas under the eaves. It is not good for art studios or other work spaces requiring easy-to-clean surfaces, however. In these situations, vinyl, wood, or ceramic tiles would be better. If you use tile in the attic, be sure the floor is stable.

Wall and ceiling materials

Most ceilings and walls are covered with wallboard and then finished with paint, paneling, wallcovering, or other coverings. Attics present an interesting design challenge because they often have dramatic and unusual shapes, sometimes with no delineation between the wall and the ceiling.

It may be more difficult to install materials in an attic than in other rooms, especially large panels of wallboard or paneling. But the job should go smoothly if you have plenty of help.

The following guidelines will help you to select your finish materials.
☐ Use plain, light-colored wallcoverings or paint to make the unusual angles and shapes interesting but not dominating.
☐ Use patterned coverings, applied to all surfaces in the same direction, to disguise or draw attention away from angles.
☐ Use bold, contrasting colors and patterns to make the unusual angles a focus of interest.
☐ Use patterns with vertical lines to make walls look higher and wide spaces narrower.
☐ Use horizontal patterns to make a room feel wider.
☐ If you are using wallcovering in an attic with a sloped ceiling and no walls, apply it only to the bottom of the wall to make the room feel larger. This will also help alleviate the feeling that the walls are caving in.
☐ Always apply paneling over wallboard, not directly to the framing.
☐ Leave rafters, beams, or other framing members exposed for interesting effects. If they are not attractive enough to harmonize with other finished surfaces, cover them with finish lumber or wallboard.

Trim and fixtures

You may have a designer or architect make all your selections for you, but you will probably want to voice your preferences for trim, electrical fixtures, doors, hardware, and plumbing fixtures.

There are no special guidelines for choosing these materials. Cost will certainly be an important factor. The prices of doors range from $35 to $350; trim costs can vary from $.35 a foot to more than $2.50 a foot; a light fixture could be $45 or $450.

Whatever your choices, maintain a consistent look throughout each room and, when in doubt, choose simple, well-made materials.

Is there good lighting?

A well-planned lighting system does not merely illuminate space, it makes it enchanting. Illuminating an attic is no different from lighting a conventional room, although the limited headroom might prevent the use of suspended ceiling fixtures. Also, insufficient rafter depth and required ceiling insulation may make it impossible to use recessed fixtures. Codes usually specify a 3-inch clearance between insulation and fixtures. If recessing fixtures in the ceiling is not an option, consider using surface-mounted fixtures, track lighting, or wall-mounted fixtures.

Plan the lighting system during the design phase of your project, not after the room is finished. Consulting with your architect, an interior designer, or a lighting specialist will pay off richly when you see how modern lighting techniques are able to bring drama, excitement, and beauty to your attic.

As with any interior design, attic lighting should include the following.

General illumination. You can best achieve general lighting with indirect fixtures that cast a warm glow over large areas. Use recessed ceiling fixtures, wall sconces that wash a wall, or floor-mounted spotlights to illuminate the sloped ceiling. Hanging fixtures from a vaulted ceiling may also be appropriate.

Task lighting. This will be needed to focus on counters, desks, reading areas, or work tables. Use spotlights or recessed canisters.

Accent lighting. Accent lighting is usually aimed at specific objects or architectural features. The effect can be achieved with spotlights, wall sconces, or recessed canisters.

Lighting

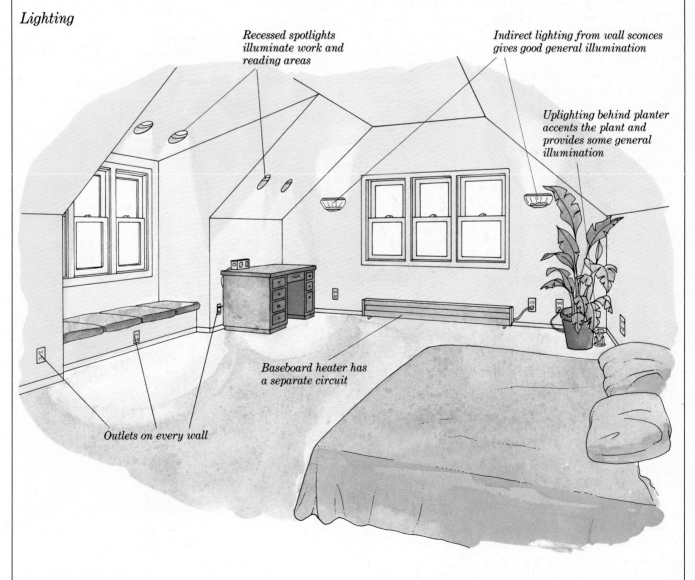

Recessed spotlights
illuminate work and
reading areas

Indirect lighting from wall sconces
gives good general illumination

Uplighting behind planter
accents the plant and
provides some general
illumination

Baseboard heater has
a separate circuit

Outlets on every wall

What special elements can be added?

Some features add appeal even if they do not solve any specific design problems. You may want to consider using some in your attic.

Bear in mind, however, that a successful design depends more on a unified, harmonious feeling than on the use of particular devices. Each surface, each piece of furniture, and each fixture should blend with the rest, satisfy the particular need, and contribute to the overall feeling of the space. If you can blend these special elements, you will make your attic especially appealing.

Balcony or deck

Whether you want to greet the morning sun, catch a breath of fresh air, or sit and watch the world go by, an upstairs balcony adds appeal to any attic room. The ideal balcony faces south (except in extremely hot climates), is shaded by a roof overhang or trees in the summer, overlooks an interesting garden, has privacy, and is easy to step out onto. It need not be spacious—just large enough for two chairs and a small table.

A small balcony, or even a large deck, can be attached to a gable wall at the end of an attic. This wall will have enough room for a door, possibly a double French door or sliding glass door. A small balcony can also be added to the front of a dormer where it will be sheltered by the dormer roof.

Windows

Like any new living space, an attic needs natural light and ventilation. But an attic offers much more potential for interesting windows than most other rooms. It is high enough for sweeping panoramas, or at least closeup views of the treetop world. Windows can also be placed almost anywhere, thanks to skylights and roof windows.

Attic windows do not necessarily have to resemble those in the rest of the house. Attic walls often have irregular shapes that are suitable for nonstandard window treatments. For example, a small, round window fits perfectly into the top of a gable wall for an interesting focal point. A large, curved window can sweep across one end of the attic for a dramatic flare that frames a spectacular view. A curved window can top a rectangular window. You can also fit windows into the odd corners and angles of an attic, or you can install a series of square windows in a pyramid.

Bathrooms

An extra bathroom, always a welcome convenience, is essential in some attic conversions, such as an apartment, a master suite, or a guest room. Even a tiny half-bath is better than trudging up and down stairs. And the cost and effort required to squeeze in a bathroom will correspond to a rise in the resale value of your home.

Nooks and alcoves

Attics have a special quality most people associate with quiet retreats and private getaways. They are often described as cozy, warm, charming, and intimate, all of which stem from the huddled, protected feeling evoked by sloped ceilings and narrow spaces.

Nooks and alcoves help to create this feeling, and it is likely your attic already has some if your plans include a dormer or your roof has intersecting ridgelines. If not, you can create them quite easily. One way is to interrupt a long kneewall

A tub can slide easily into the space under a dormer, which, because of insufficient headroom, might otherwise be wasted.

with an open space recessed back under the eaves.

Another way to break up a wall is with a closet or small bathroom that extends out into the room, creating alcoves on each side.

A third way is to build a tiny loft, if there is enough headroom, creating alcoves both above and below.

Built-in seating

Built-in seating adds charm to an attic, increases usable floor space, and provides storage. A wide seat tucked into a nook or a bench built into a corner can double as a bed.

Built-ins offer a wonderful opportunity for displaying your decorating talents: A single, neat cushion covered with crisp patterned fabric has a smart and trim appearance; an overstuffed mattress covered with rich fabric and piled with brightly colored pillows suggests opulence. Whatever your tastes, you can create a sitting area that tempts one to stay awhile.

Platforms

Attics are good places to use raised platforms covered with the same carpeting as the floor. They reduce the need for furnishings and are less likely to interrupt traffic patterns than they might be in more centrally located rooms.

Fireplaces

Fireplaces and stoves are relatively easy to install in attics because the chimney pipe is short and only has the roof to penetrate. Many small units are available that are just right for an attic already warmed by the rest of the house.

The sharp pitch of the roof offers low but deep space that can be used as an out-of-season clothes closet.

Are you ready to begin construction?

The completed design includes a set of working drawings, specification lists, materials lists, and related documents. See page 14 for a listing of these documents. They are the basis of the construction phase.

Once the design is finished and permits have been issued, you are ready to begin construction.

Some of the work in an attic conversion is similar to any other type of home-improvement project. This is true of window and door installations, plumbing, wiring, wallboard, finish work, flooring, and painting. For techniques and more information about these skills, refer to *Ortho's Home Improvement Encyclopedia* or Ortho's library of books on specific home-improvement topics.

Whether you hire professionals or do some of the work yourself, review the information on the next pages, as well as the following guidelines.

☐ Avoid starting the project during the warmest season. An attic can be unbearably hot until windows and insulation are installed.

☐ If new or rebuilt stairs are required, rough them in as soon as possible. Hold off on the finish for the treads, such as carpet or hardwood flooring, until the end of the project.

☐ If you are building a dormer or installing large windows, delay closing up the opening until most of the attic is completed. Use the opening for hoisting in large materials, such as lumber or wallboard, and for lowering debris.

☐ If the stairwell does not have a door, seal off the opening with a tarp or plastic sheeting to control dust.

☐ Ensure that the walls supporting the attic floor or any part of the roof have continuous support straight down to the foundation or piers.

CONSTRUCTION TECHNIQUES

An attic conversion includes techniques that are rarely used elsewhere. The following section presents instructions for doing most of these tasks.

Installing floor joists

Install additional joists of the same size, either next to the existing joists or between them. This is possible when the existing joists are at least 2 by 6s, and there are no obstructions, such as wiring or plaster keys, to keep the new joists from sitting flush on the wall plates.

The floor will be stronger if you nail the new joists into the existing joists—using 12-penny (12d) nails, 16 inches on center—so both have maximum stiffness. Keep in mind that nailing into the existing joists may jar plaster loose from the ceiling below.

Building a new floor. When there are too many obstructions to place new joists of equal size next to the existing joists, or the ceiling below is vulnerable to hammering vibrations, it is better to build a completely new floor system independent of the existing ceiling joists.

Install new joists on 12- or 16-inch centers. Place them on spacers nailed into the top plates of the bearing walls. The spacers should be thick enough to clear the ceiling and any other obstruction, such as wiring, by at least ¾ inch; 2 by 4s are commonly used. You may also need to install blocking or bridging between the joists as required for conventional floor framing (over bearing walls or beams and at the midpoint of any span of 16 feet or more).

Reducing the span. You can also strengthen a floor by reducing the spans for the existing joists. Do this by installing a beam or new bearing wall beneath them. This will interrupt the living space below, however. The new bearing wall or any posts supporting the beam must have continuous support down to the foundation wall or foundation piers.

This type of support is practical only when you are planning to alter the downstairs living space also.

Getting new joists into the attic

If your project requires adding new joists, the most difficult task may be getting the joists into the attic.

Sometimes the easist method is to strip away a long section of roofing at the eaves and slide the joists in from the roof or from scaffolding erected outside the building. This method also makes it easier to trim the top corners of the joists to fit beneath the sloped roof sheathing and to nail the joists into the top plates at the eaves.

Installing the subfloor

The subfloor is installed over the floor joists only after all wiring, plumbing, mechanical, and insulation work has been completed and inspected.

The strongest type of subfloor is plywood, usually CDX, at least ⅝ inch thick, with tongue-and-groove edges. Sometimes various types of particle board are used, or even 1-by boards laid diagonally across the joists.

If the finish floor is to be resilient tile or sheet vinyl, use CDX plywood that is plugged and touch sanded (PTS), or install ¼-inch hardboard rough side up over the subfloor.

Lay the subfloor panels perpendicular to the joists, staggering the ends by 4 feet. Leave 1/16- to 1/8-inch gaps between panels. To eliminate squeaks, attach the panels with construction adhesive as well as 8d ring-shank nails. Space the nails every 6 inches around the perimeter and every 10 inches within the panel.

Subfloor

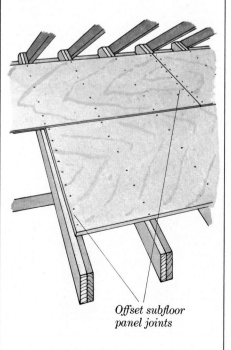

Offset subfloor panel joints

Additional joists

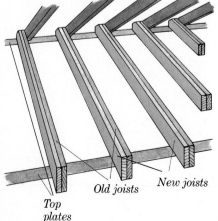

Old joists *New joists* *Top plates*

New floor

Spacers *New joists* *Top plates* *Old joists*

Altering roof framing

Always seek professional advice about changing roof framing, and leave extensive work, such as changing the pitch, to them. However, the following operations can be done by homeowners with carpentry skills.

Raising collar ties

When collar ties are a few inches too low for proper headroom, you can raise them, one or two at a time. The old ties will be brittle and tough, so replace them with new lumber (2 by 4s or 2 by 6s).

Nail each new tie to the rafters with three 16d nails at each end. For a flat ceiling, attach new ceiling material directly to them.

Removing collar ties

There are several methods for removing collar ties.

Removing some ties. You can remove only some of the ties, but the remaining ones should be no more than 4 feet apart and at least 80 inches above the finish floor. Normal practice is to leave a collar tie on every third pair of rafters.

Removing all ties. If you do this, the bottoms of the rafters must be nailed directly into the attic floor joists, not just the wall plates. Also, there should be a continuous ridge board connecting the tops of the rafters. If not, install blocking between the rafters along the ridge before removing collar ties.

Before removing ties, make sure the rafters are large enough for the entire span (consult rafter span table). If not, support them with kneewalls or purlins, or double up the existing rafters with new rafters. This may be necessary anyway to create enough space for insulation. However, when you install deeper rafters, the bottoms will not make full contact with the wall plates; therefore they are considered only as strong as the old rafters.

Installing new rafters

To install new rafters, first make templates for cutting the top and bottom plates for cutting the top and bottom angle of each rafter, or set a bevel gauge for these angles. Measure each rafter length along the roof sheathing. Mark and cut the new rafter. Set the top in place and slide the bottom onto the wall plate.

If the roof sags you will need a jack to raise the roof enough to slide the rafter bottom onto the plate. Set the jack on planks that span at least three floor joists. Place it under the center of the original rafter and lift very slowly. You may need a second jack to lift the new rafter onto the plate.

When the rafter is in place, nail it into the original rafter with 16d nails spaced every 12 inches. Toenail the rafter into the plate with 8d nails.

Installing a new rafter

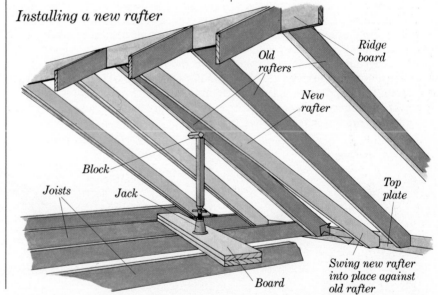

Old rafters · Ridge board · New rafter · Block · Joists · Jack · Top plate · Swing new rafter into place against old rafter · Board

High slope rafters

Allowable spans only for slope greater than 3 in 12; 30 pounds per square foot live loads (supporting wallboard ceiling and heavy roof covering). Listed in feet and inches.

Rafter size	Rafter spacing	Allowable extreme fiber stress in bending F_b psi														
		500	600	700	800	900	1000	1100	1200	1300	1400	1500	1600	1700	1800	1900
2x4	16 o.c.	4-1	4-6	4-11	5-3	5-6	5-10	6-1	6-5	6-8	6-11	7-2	7-5	7-7	7-10	8-0
	24 o.c.	3-4	3-8	4-0	4-3	4-6	4-9	5-0	5-3	5-5	5-8	5-10	6-0	6-3	6-5	6-7
2x6	16 o.c.	6-6	7-1	7-8	8-2	8-8	9-2	9-7	10-0	10-5	10-10	11-3	11-7	11-11	12-4	12-8
	24 o.c.	5-4	5-10	6-3	6-8	7-1	7-6	7-10	8-2	8-6	8-10	9-2	9-6	9-9	10-0	10-4
2x8	16 o.c.	8-7	9-4	10-1	10-10	11-6	12-1	12-8	13-3	13-9	14-4	14-10	15-3	15-9	16-3	16-8
	24 o.c.	7-0	7-8	8-3	8-10	9-4	9-10	10-4	10-10	11-3	11-8	12-1	12-6	12-10	13-3	13-7
2x10	16 o.c.	10-11	11-11	12-11	13-9	14-8	15-5	16-2	16-11	17-7	18-3	18-11	19-6	20-1	20-8	21-3
	24 o.c.	8-11	9-9	10-6	11-3	11-11	12-7	13-2	13-9	14-4	13-11	15-5	15-11	16-5	16-11	17-4

Raising or removing an attic ceiling

If you have a finished attic ceiling that is too low, you can raise it or remove it altogether. Although it is safe to remove the finished ceiling—usually just wallboard or lath and plaster—you must be careful about disturbing ceiling joists or other framing that are acting as collar ties. When in doubt, assume that all joists are collar ties, and remove them using the method described on page 51.

Building a dormer

Many dormers are complex but, with basic carpentry skills and some experience with rafters, you should be able to build this simple dormer.

Your plans will indicate the size and roof slope of the dormer. They will also show where the roof needs to be reinforced with double rafters or other framing. If the dormer is large, or if you are building in an area that gets a lot of snow, you may also have to add a reinforced ridge beam.

This dormer has the front wall set back from the house wall for a more pleasing appearance, but the attic floor must be reinforced. It is more common to remove the rafters all the way to the downstairs wall and then set the dormer wall directly on top of the house wall.

Lay out the opening. Make sure the attic floor is adequately supported and covered with subflooring. Lay out the dormer dimensions on the floor, then hold a plumb bob over each corner and mark where the line hits the roof. These marks are the corners of the roof opening. Drill holes or drive nails through these marks so they will be seen from the roof. Double the rafters on either side of the proposed opening, using the same techniques as described for installing new roof rafters.

Cut the rafters. Remove the roofing between the marks and about 12 inches beyond. Snap chalk lines on top of the roof sheathing between the marks, cut along them, and remove the sheathing between them. Brace the rafters before cutting and mark each rafter as shown. Try to make the top cut square to the dormer rafters and the bottom cut plumb. Have a helper hold each rafter as you cut it, setting it down gently so as not to jar the ceiling below. Do not remove the braces until you install double headers to hold the cut rafters.

Support the headers by nailing 3-inch joist hangers to the double rafters at each corner of the opening. Slide the first header into the hangers and nail it into all the cut rafter ends; then install the second piece.

Build the front wall. Frame the wall on the floor, so the corner studs fit snugly between the double rafters and the top plates extend 3½ inches beyond them at both ends.

Stand the wall up and set it in place. Nail a diagonal brace to it, plumb the wall, and secure the brace to a block nailed into the floor. Nail the soleplate into the floor, at the joists. Then toenail the studs into the header and facenail them into the double rafters.

Removing rafters

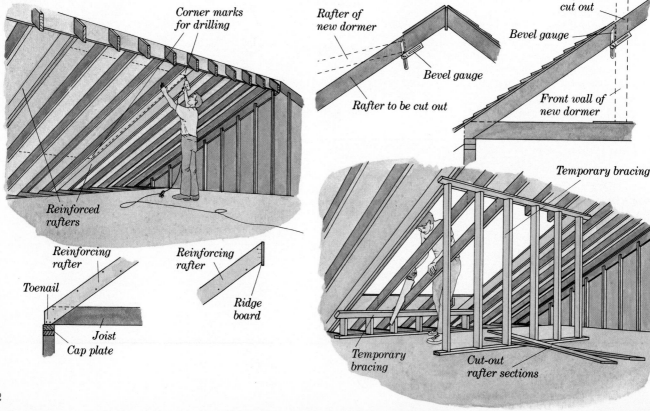

Corner marks for drilling

Reinforced rafters

Reinforcing rafter

Toenail

Joist

Cap plate

Reinforcing rafter

Ridge board

Rafter of new dormer

Bevel gauge

Rafter to be cut out

Rafter to be cut out

Bevel gauge

Front wall of new dormer

Temporary bracing

Temporary bracing

Cut-out rafter sections

Install corner posts. Build corner posts for the wall with two 2 by 4s and scraps of ⅜-inch plywood. Measure them to fit between the top plate of the new wall and the exposed roof sheathing, cutting the bottoms at the same angle as the roofline. Set each of the posts in place, check for plumb, and toenail them into the rafters, wall studs, and top plate.

Install the rafters. Cut rafters from lumber sized for the span, usually 2 by 6 or 2 by 8. Mark the angle of the top cut by holding the rafter stock so the top end butts up against the double header. Have a helper hold the other end of the board against the side of the new corner post so its bottom edge is at the same height as the top inside edge of the cap plate. Mark the board by scribing a line parallel to the face of the header.

Cut on this line, put the board back in the same position, trace cutout marks for the bird's mouth on it, and cut the notch. Test this rafter, make corrections, and use it as a pattern to cut all others except the outside two.

Lay out the rafter locations along the cap plate and header, 16 or 24 inches on center, depending on the span. Secure the top ends of rafters to the double header with joist hangers. Secure the bottom ends by toenailing into the cap plate. The tops of the two outside rafters should be angled to fit against the roofline. Close in the dormer by framing the end walls and installing sheathing, roofing, siding, and windows.

Installing new rafters and walls

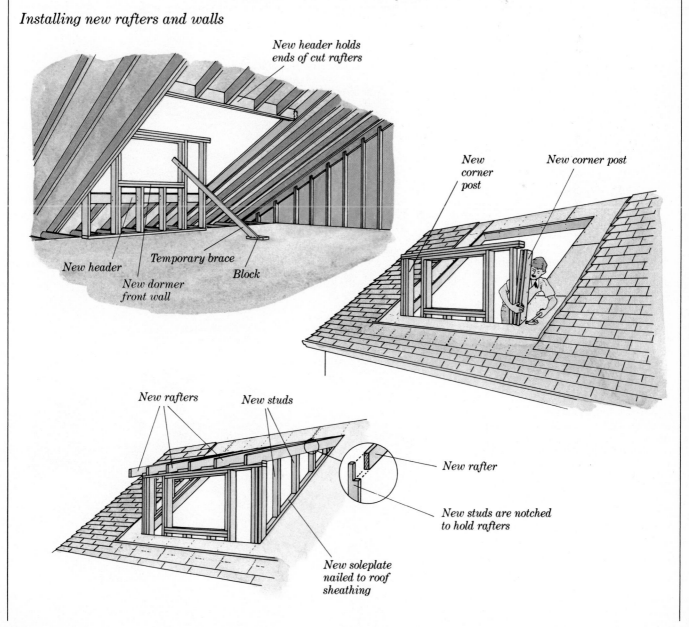

New header holds ends of cut rafters

New header

New dormer front wall

Temporary brace

Block

New corner post

New corner post

New rafters

New studs

New rafter

New studs are notched to hold rafters

New soleplate nailed to roof sheathing

Building stairs

Complex or ornate stairs are beyond the skills of most homeowners (and most carpenters). But a conventional, straight-run stairway is something you may be able to take on if you are doing the attic conversion yourself. Be sure to check all local code requirements first (see page 36).

Calculating stair dimensions

1. Measure the vertical distance from floor to floor, allowing for the thickness of finish floor materials.
2. Divide this distance by 7 to get the approximate number of steps. Round the answer to the next whole number and divide that number into the original measurement. The answer will be 7 plus a fraction. It represents the height of each riser if they are all to be exactly the same.
Example: $108'' \div 7 = 15.4$ steps
$108'' \div 16$ steps $= 7.2''$
Riser $= 7^3/_{16}''$
3. To find the tread width, subtract the riser dimension from 17½ inches.
Example: $17^8/_{16}'' - 7^3/_{16}''$
Tread $= 10^5/_{16}''$

Preparing the rough opening

If the opening runs parallel to the joists, cut through only one or two joists and support the cut ends with double headers. If the opening is perpendicular to the joists, many must be cut. Support them with double headers, a new wall, or a beam.

Support the ceiling from below with temporary bracing.

Lay out the stairwell dimensions on the attic floor and remove the old flooring from inside the marks. Mark the ceiling for cutting, allowing room for framing, finish materials, and handrails.

Remove the ceiling and cut the joists from above.

Frame the opening by nailing trimmer joists to the end joists with 16d nails, 12 inches on center. Nail the double headers the same way.

Make sure the joists are supported at both ends.

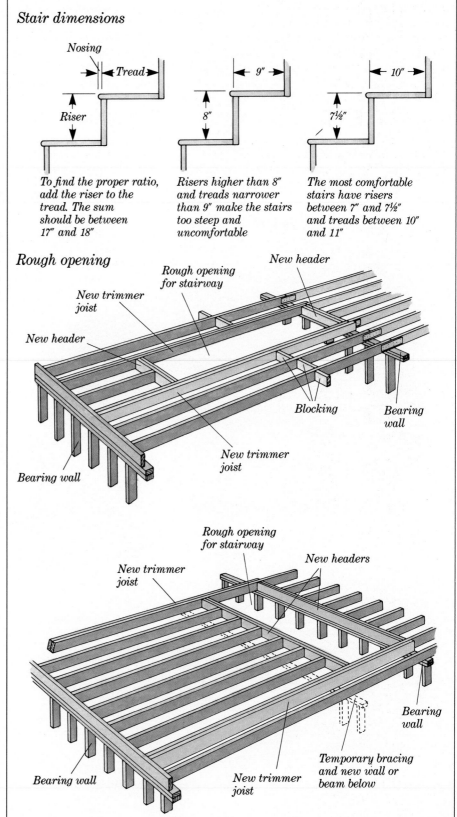

Stair dimensions

Nosing
Tread
Riser

To find the proper ratio, add the riser to the tread. The sum should be between 17″ and 18″

9″
8″

Risers higher than 8″ and treads narrower than 9″ make the stairs too steep and uncomfortable

10″
7½″

The most comfortable stairs have risers between 7″ and 7½″ and treads between 10″ and 11″

Rough opening

Rough opening for stairway
New header
New trimmer joist
New header
Blocking
Bearing wall
New trimmer joist
Bearing wall

Rough opening for stairway
New trimmer joist
New headers
Bearing wall
Bearing wall
New trimmer joist
Temporary bracing and new wall or beam below

Installing the stairs

Use straight 2 by 12 stock for the stringers. To mark the cuts for the first stringer, set a framing square so the tongue (short leg) intersects the top edge of the board at the riser dimension and the blade does so at the tread dimension. Scribe the outline of the square on the wood.

Slide the square along the board so it lines up the same way, intersecting the original outline. Scribe again and continue until all steps are laid out.

Cut the stringers. To make the bottom step the same height as the others, trim the bottom of the stringer by the thickness of one tread. Then cut a notch for a 2 by 4 cleat.

Place the stringer in the rough opening to see if it fits properly. Make adjustments and then use it as a pattern to cut the second stringer. Stairways wider than 32 inches will require a third stringer.

Install the stringers, using a ledger or joist hangers at the top. If you nail one stringer to wall framing, add a 2 by 4 to make a space for wallboard and finish trim.

Cut risers from 1-by lumber or ¾-inch plywood and install them.

Cut treads from special tread stock with a rounded nosing. Rip it to a width equal to your tread dimension plus the thickness of the tread stock.

Attach the treads with construction adhesive and ring-shank nails. Face-nail the treads into the stringers and drive nails from the back of the risers into the treads.

Cutting stringers

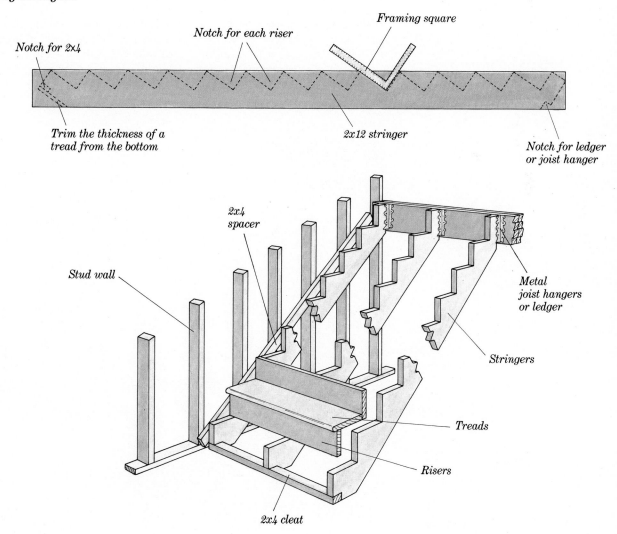

Notch for 2x4

Notch for each riser

Framing square

Trim the thickness of a tread from the bottom

2x12 stringer

Notch for ledger or joist hanger

2x4 spacer

Stud wall

Metal joist hangers or ledger

Stringers

Treads

Risers

2x4 cleat

Framing walls and ceilings

Framing for attic walls and ceilings is similar to other framing except for the irregular angles and heights. Kneewalls are short walls that fit under the roof eaves. Partition walls divide the attic into rooms, and are full height in the center but sloped at each end to conform to the pitch.

Building kneewalls

Codes specify the minimum height of kneewalls, typically 4 feet. This makes it convenient for installing panels of wallboard horizontally. However, you may want higher walls so the tallest person in your family can stand comfortably within 3 feet of them. If the walls are 5 feet high, use 4 by 10 wallboard panels cut in half. You may also want to frame openings in the walls for recessed shelves or built-in cabinets.

To build a kneewall. Cut a 2 by 4 soleplate the length of the new wall. Temporarily place it in position on the subfloor. Drop a plumb bob from one edge of each rafter so it aligns with one edge of the soleplate. Mark the location on both the rafter and soleplate. This way you will know where to place the stud. To ascertain the length of the stud, measure the distance along the plumb line between the rafter and plate.

If the measurements vary by less than ¼ inch. Cut equal-length studs that are long enough to lap against the sides of the rafters. Square-cut the ends. Lay the studs on the floor and facenail the soleplate into the bottom of each stud with two 16d nails.

Raise the wall into place and nail through the soleplate into the floor joists. Plumb each stud and nail it onto the rafter with three 10d nails.

If the measurements vary by more than ¼ inch. You may be able to take the sag out of the rafters by cutting all studs at an angle so they can be jammed under the rafters and toenailed in place.

To do this, nail the soleplate to the subfloor. Cut all studs the same length; use a bevel gauge to mark the top angle. Toenail each stud to the soleplate and the rafter.

Because there is no top plate, you need a nailing surface for wallboard or paneling. Cut and toenail short lengths of 2 by 4 between the studs.

Kneewall construction

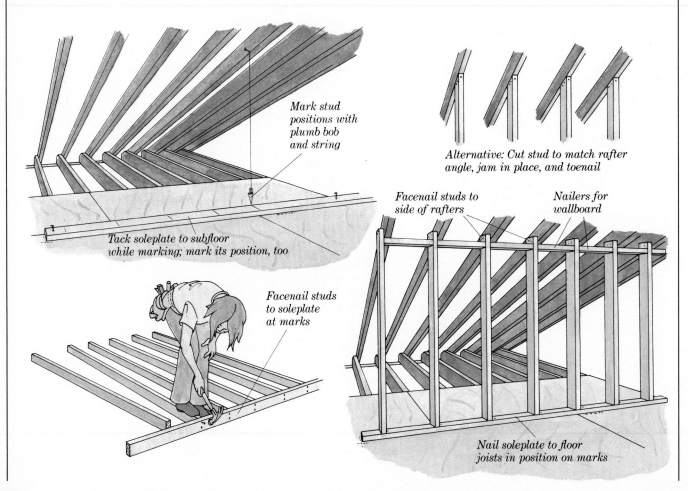

Mark stud positions with plumb bob and string

Tack soleplate to subfloor while marking; mark its position, too

Facenail studs to soleplate at marks

Alternative: Cut stud to match rafter angle, jam in place, and toenail

Facenail studs to side of rafters

Nailers for wallboard

Nail soleplate to floor joists in position on marks

Installing ceiling joists

For a level ceiling, install joists between the rafters. Mark the location of each joist on the rafters by measuring up from the subfloor along a plumb line. Add the finish floor and ceiling dimensions to the ceiling height (7½ feet minimum).

Use 2 by 4s or 2 by 6s for the joists, depending on the span. Cut both ends at the same angle as the slope of the roof to provide the maximum nailing surface, allowing at least ¼ inch clearance at each end.

Lift each joist (crown side up if it is bowed) and tack one end to the rafter with a 16d nail. Check for level and finish nailing both ends.

Erecting end walls

Cut a soleplate to fit between the two kneewalls and nail it in place. Try to locate it beneath a ceiling joist. Cut the horizontal top plate and nail it directly into a joist. If the wall falls between two joists, nail blocking between the joists and nail the top plate to the blocking.

Alternatively, you can install the blocking ¾ inch above the bottom of the joists and nail a 1 by 6 to the blocking before installing the top plate.

Nail the top plate to the 1 by 6. Install sloping top plates between the kneewalls and horizontal top plate. Nail them into rafters or to blocking installed between them.

Mark the stud locations along the soleplate. Measure for each stud along a plumb line, cut it, and toenail it in place. Cut the tops of studs at the same angle as the roof. Plumb each stud with a level before nailing.

Completing the project

Next to the planning and design stage, the homestretch is the most critical phase of any project. It is the time when fatigue, impatience, disappointment, and misunderstanding are most likely to develop. But this need not happen. Patience, thorough planning, and a firm commitment to see the project through will go a long way toward preventing these sour notes. Prepare yourself by being ready for the following.

The scope of the project. There is a lot of tedious and time-consuming work toward the end. When the wallboard is up, it may seem like the project is nearly finished, but in reality that is only the halfway point.

Legal problems. Know how to take legal procedures to end a contract. Require lien releases from any subcontractors or the general contractor, a final clearance from the building inspector, and your own satisfaction before making final payments.

Moving in. Avoid annoyance and frustration by completing all work before moving into your new rooms.

Final celebration. Plan a party, vacation, formal moving-in day, or similar event to mark the end of your project. This may seem like an unnecessary extravagance, but it is important to acknowledge (and reward) the efforts of everyone involved—especially yourself!

End wall construction

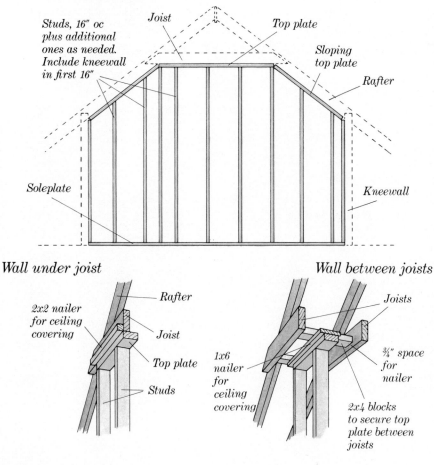

Studs, 16" oc plus additional ones as needed. Include kneewall in first 16"

Joist

Top plate

Sloping top plate

Rafter

Soleplate

Kneewall

Wall under joist

2x2 nailer for ceiling covering

Rafter

Joist

Top plate

Studs

Wall between joists

Joists

1x6 nailer for ceiling covering

¾" space for nailer

2x4 blocks to secure top plate between joists

THE LOWDOWN ON BASEMENTS

E very year thousands of homes are built with unfinished basements. If you own such a home, you may have been using your basement as a storage area, a utility center, or an informal game room. A basement is ideal for such uses: It is usually fairly big; it is out of the way; and the floor is solid.

If you have more ambitious plans for your basement and wish to convert it into pleasant living space, you will find that many features will create a challenge. The room is naturally dark; the ceiling is low and often has pipes and ducts hanging from it; the walls are rough and sometimes damp; the floor is hard (or does not exist); posts and utility equipment clutter the space; limited window area exaggerates the drab walls.

Many of these problems can be eliminated or concealed. Others may actually be blessings in disguise if you view them as design assets rather than as liabilities.

The following pages illustrate possibilities for your basement. They show how some of these drawbacks can be overcome and how problems can be turned into opportunities for adapting a basement to almost any use. With thoughtful design and careful attention to detail, your basement can be as inviting and attractive as any room in your home.

This basement retreat is surrounded by a quaint garden path, vibrant hanging fuchsias, and a border of agapanthuses. Well-placed windows can offer scenic ground-level views—added bonuses to basement living.

EXPLORING POSSIBILITIES

M*ost basements are large enough for more than one use; many can become several rooms. However, you do not need a large, rambling basement to create more living space. All you need is a dry space with enough headroom.*

If the space is limited and you have more than one use in mind, it may be possible to use the same room for several activities. When deciding what can go together in one room, try to combine opposites, such as an active use with a passive one, or a daytime use with a different nighttime one. An example of an active and passive use combination is a laundry combined with a place for reading or conversation. An example of different uses at different times of day would be to combine a daytime office with a bedroom. These examples may not work in your home, and it is unlikely that two activities can occur simultaneously, but you can create a space that will accommodate both.

When planning a room for multiple uses, make sure the scheme will serve each purpose well. When combining a laundry with a study, provide counter space on which to fold clothes as well as to spread out papers and books. Likewise, a space intended for both quiet reading and the pursuit of a hobby should have a tranquil and uncluttered feeling as well as plenty of storage and work surfaces. It may be necessary to divide a multipurpose room physically or to equip it with flexible furnishings in order to accommodate both uses.

Family rooms

Basements are often used as family rooms because they are remote, have abundant space, and can be arranged and adapted as the family grows. Very often they lie idle and neglected because the space is unappealing, or because it is not planned for a specific use. Your family room will be more successful if you plan it carefully, accounting for all possible uses. You may want to make a large, single room for a variety of uses, or separate rooms, each one devoted to a specific use such as a media center.

For a family room, consider:
☐ A cheery atmosphere with south-facing windows
☐ Comfortable seating for eight or more people, arranged in a conversational grouping with no more than 8 feet between any two people

□ Tables and counters for games, hobbies, and eating

□ A quiet corner for a study desk

□ A minikitchen, or facilities for preparing light snacks including a sink, refrigerator, and a small counter

Media rooms

The remote location, limited window area, low ceilings, and comfortable year-round temperature make a basement ideal for a media room.

For a media room, consider:

□ Comfortable seating for TV viewers at an angle of no more than 45 degrees to the screen, no farther away than 10 to 12 feet

□ Shelving and storage flexible enough for various sizes of equipment; cabinets with doors to provide security and prevent dust gathering; a small fan to prevent overheating of equipment

□ Plenty of electrical outlets, with surge protection against damage from lightning or other charges

□ Wiring for special uses, such as speaker wires or cable hookups

□ Sound insulation in the walls, ceiling, and door if you do not want to hear loud music upstairs

□ Windows free of sunlight or glare

□ Portable snack tables

Solarium panels flood the basement with light and provide a view of the garden.

Well-lit display cases make this storage wall a point of interest in a family room.

Rooms for formal entertaining

If getting your home ready for guests is a major project, what you may need is a separate area that is always ready for entertaining. Consider your basement. Imagine it transformed into a dazzling showcase with curved walls, sculptured ceiling surfaces, dramatic lighting, a convenient serving center, a sweeping staircase, and designer furnishings. People do not generally consider putting basements to such a use, and it will require a sensitive design to be successful. But a basement does not have to be informal; it can have as much glamour and appeal as any other room.

For a formal entertaining room, consider:

☐ A wide, inviting stairway leading into the room and convenient to the front entry
☐ A formal serving area for food and drinks
☐ A dramatic focal point, such as a fireplace or picture window
☐ A large central area
☐ Alcoves for intimate seating and conversation

Playrooms

A playroom is an excellent use of basement space. The low ceiling, high windows, and intruding posts are hardly noticed by youngsters at play. The solid floor and walls can stand any abuse. A basement is not usually subject to drafts, and noise can be controlled.

For a playroom, consider:

☐ Spacious, uncluttered floors
☐ Carpeting that is soft but stain and wear resistant
☐ A clear view of the area from other rooms to facilitate supervision of children's play
☐ A flexible design so the room can be adapted to future needs

Offices

The isolation and privacy of a basement make it an ideal place for a quiet getaway, whether for disciplined work or for relaxation. Although no basement living space should have moisture problems, it is especially important that an office or den be absolutely dry because books and documents are vulnerable to moisture damage.

Suggested space requirements are: 64 square feet of floor area for desk, chair, file cabinet, and typing table
30-inch-high desk
30-inch-deep desk
8- to 12-inch-deep shelves
26-inch-high typing/computer table
36-inch-high counters
42-inch space in front of file cabinets
36-inch space in front of bookcases

For an office, consider:

☐ An outside entrance or easy access for visitors
☐ Sound insulation to deaden noise from overhead as well as from a furnace, air conditioner, or laundry appliances
☐ Clean, uncluttered surfaces
☐ Comfortable seating for reading or conferences, with natural light
☐ Direct lighting over work areas
☐ A business or use permit from your city, if required

The way a place is furnished determines its use. Therefore, you can entertain formally even in a basement when it contains a wood ceiling, a stone-faced fireplace wall, and elegant upholstery.

Sheer exuberance of shape and color are what makes this space work. Rather than being obscured, the duct has been painted a bright green. Stamped tin ceiling tiles from the Victorian era combine unabashedly with modern art and cushions in Mondrianesque colors.

Above: A solarium transforms a dark basement into a sunlit garden room in which to tend plants or stretch out on the mattressed platform with a good book.

Opposite: People upstairs can see who's playing pool as easily as those downstairs around the fire. This dramatic basement space is open to, as well as lit by, windows on the upper floor.

Hobby rooms

A basement is particularly suited to creative hobbies that require an out-of-the-way location, durable surfaces, and space in which to work. A basement room can be furnished as an attractive place in which to display models that you have made or to practice a musical instrument.

For a hobby room, consider:
☐ Easy-to-clean floors and surfaces
☐ Enough ventilation to remove any noxious paint or glue fumes
☐ Humidity control and shading to protect artwork
☐ Cabinets with locks to keep dangerous materials out of reach
☐ A sink
☐ A separate entrance for delivery of large supplies

Recreation rooms

It is hard to imagine a space better suited for a recreation room than a basement. The remote location means that noise can be contained; the large size of most basements creates a flexible space for almost any activity; and it is certainly not difficult to create an informal atmosphere. A recreation room can easily be combined with a fitness center.

For a recreation room, consider:
☐ A space at least 12 feet by 16 feet
☐ Sound insulation in the ceiling and stairwell
☐ Zoned areas for quiet activities and noisy activities
☐ Built-in seating along one wall

Apartments

Local zoning and building laws vary widely, so check your own to see if secondary units are allowed and what regulations apply.

Permission for a separate apartment is often based on lot size, floor area, number of bedrooms, availability of separate utility meters, respect for neighbors' privacy, maximum number of occupants, and the installation of special fire precautions.

Workshops

The dream of every do-it-yourselfer is a complete workshop: a space in which to organize tools and work on projects that do not have to be cleared away whenever you are not working on them. A basement is the ideal location because it is easier to heat than a garage and humidity can be controlled. Noisy power tools will not disturb the rest of the family, and you do not have to share the space with cars and bicycles.

For a workshop, consider:

☐ Switches or circuit breakers with locks to control all equipment
☐ Locked storage for all hazardous materials
☐ Bright, even lighting
☐ Light-colored walls
☐ Fire extinguisher
☐ An area with openable windows for good ventilation
☐ A separate outside entrance for bringing in large materials
☐ Electrical outlets in the ceiling for plugging in stationary power tools
☐ Tool storage on walls, suspended from ceiling, and under benches
☐ A separate storeroom for lumber
☐ Workbenches on lockable casters
☐ Separate zones for workbenches, portable tools, and stationary ones
☐ A floor covering that is soft underfoot, such as wood or heavy vinyl
☐ Weather stripping on the doors for noise and dust control
☐ A central vacuum system for cleaning up sawdust

Above: *If a basement is to be used as an apartment or for entertaining, you will need a kitchen, even if it is small. Here the strong architectural features and the tiled walls make the food-preparation area a dramatic focal point in an open space.*

Opposite: *Strong, graphic lines in the rug, tiled wall, brick hearth, and slatted ceiling complement the architecture. This ceiling treatment could be used to hide heating and air-conditioning ducts that cannot be moved.*

Wine and food cellars

Another practical use for basements is storing wine and homemade preserves or food bought in bulk.

For a wine or food cellar, consider:

☐ Temperature control (60° to 65° F for wine)
☐ Insulated walls between cellar and heated basement spaces
☐ No direct sunlight
☐ A solid floor, free from vibrations
☐ Storage racks for organizing wine bottles and jars or cans of food
☐ Floor or shelf space for large cases of food or wine
☐ Plenty of counter space

Bedrooms

A basement is not the easiest space to convert into a bedroom, but it does have some advantages over the more traditional upstairs location. In a hot climate, the basement is often the coolest place in the house. It may also be the only space large enough for a master suite or a combination of children's bedrooms and playroom. Plumbing for an extra bathroom is often easily accessible.

For a bedroom, consider:

☐ Direct egress to the outside through a door or a window
☐ A door or window that opens from the inside with an unobstructed opening of at least 5.7 square feet
☐ Meeting local code requirements for gas or kerosene appliances, including a water heater or furnace located elsewhere in the basement
☐ A smoke alarm outside each bedroom door and over the stairs
☐ Sound insulation to deaden footsteps overhead as well as noise in a nearby stairwell or utility room
☐ Ventilation (usually an openable window area equal to one tenth of the bedroom floor area)
☐ Fences, walls, or plantings for privacy from neighbors
☐ Carpeting, if floor is concrete
☐ An outside entrance or a large picture window

Above: *If members of the family have different uses for basement space, try to accommodate them all. A person sewing in the outfitted alcove can be separated by the panel screen from other family members who are working out.*

Opposite: *For the serious oenophile, here's a cellar to dream about: Plenty of bins for bottles, a table for tastings, and walls clad in redwood.*

Fitness centers

All the family will benefit from a physical fitness room.

For a fitness center, consider:
- ☐ Exercise space as large as possible
- ☐ A bathroom with a whirlpool bath
- ☐ A sauna or steam room
- ☐ Music system
- ☐ TV for playing exercise tapes
- ☐ Well-planned ventilation

For an exercise area, consider:
- ☐ Large mirrors
- ☐ Extensive lighting on dimmers
- ☐ A padded bench or two
- ☐ A ballet bar
- ☐ A weight-lifting machine, rowing machine, or stationary bicycle

Utility spaces

Many basements already have a laundry center, often just a washer and dryer shoved against a bare concrete wall. Even though it is not convenient to upstairs bedrooms and bathrooms, a basement offers ample space for a complete laundry center.

For a laundry center, consider:
- ☐ Convenient plumbing hookups
- ☐ Wall cabinets hung above the laundry appliances
- ☐ Base cabinets with countertops
- ☐ A large sink
- ☐ A sewing center
- ☐ A built-in ironing board
- ☐ A laundry chute connected to the upstairs bedroom area

MAKING A BASEMENT LIVABLE

The goal of basement design is to plan a space that meets practical needs in a pleasant and affordable way. The path to this goal is a design process that begins by identifying your needs and priorities and ends with a set of construction documents.

Good design is a fluid and dynamic process that does not follow a rigid pattern. However, once you have established what kind of rooms you will be adding, there will be two basic design phases: The first is planning to make the basement livable, which includes evaluating the space and adapting it to meet your functional needs; the second is planning to make the basement appealing by adding finish details and considering the overall appeal of the space.

Many factors will influence your design. The most critical ones are changes needed to make the space livable, such as creating more headroom, solving moisture problems, or adding new windows.

The size and shape of your basement; the location of stairs, columns, and utility equipment; and possible locations for windows or a door will all influence the rooms you plan. There are also limitations on the placement of plumbing fixtures, heating equipment, and a fireplace.

Site factors can also influence your design: potential views, privacy from neighbors, street noise, the direction of the sun, and shade trees should all be carefully considered.

Among the first issues to consider are ceiling height and floor area. These dimensions determine the basic size and shape of the space and give you an indication of whether you need to make major structural changes.

Is there enough headroom?

Most codes require a minimum ceiling height of 7½ feet for habitable rooms (a bedroom, family room, recreation room, or kitchen) and 7 feet for hallways and bathrooms. If ducts, pipes, or other obstacles protrude below the ceiling, there should be at least 80 inches of clearance beneath them. When you measure the ceiling height in your basement be sure to allow for finish floor and ceiling materials.

Increasing headroom. Although it is possible to raise a house to increase the headroom in a basement, a more practical method is to lower the basement floor. This requires breaking out the existing concrete floor, excavating to the required depth, and pouring a new concrete floor. Leave the original foundation intact by excavating only to within 1 or 2 feet of it, then pour a concrete wall that creates a low shelf all around the room.

Doing this is a major project that involves shoring up floor beams to replace supporting columns. However, it can be worthwhile if it means that you will be able to add several hundred feet of new living space. A side benefit is that new plumbing lines and a drainage system can be installed at the same time.

Basement headroom

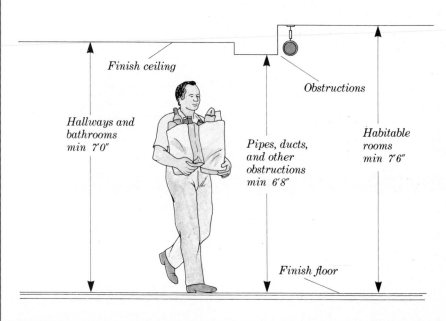

Finish ceiling

Obstructions

Hallways and bathrooms min 7'0"

Pipes, ducts, and other obstructions min 6'8"

Habitable rooms min 7'6"

Finish floor

Room sizes			
Room	Minimum floor area*	Sample size	Preferred size
Bedroom	80 sq ft	8' by 10'	11' by 14'
Master bedroom	—	—	12' by 16'
Family room	110 sq ft	10.5' by 10.5'	12' by 16'
Living room	176 sq ft	11' by 16'	12' by 18'
Other habitable room	70 sq ft	7' by 10'	—
Bathroom	35 sq ft	5' by 7'	5' by 9'
Toilet compartment	—	min. 30'' wide	—
Apartment	min. 400 sq ft		

*Floor area is defined as net floor area within enclosing walls, excluding built-in fixtures such as closets or cabinets.

Is there enough floor area?

Most basements are fairly large, with at least enough floor area for one room and usually space for more. However, if your basement is small or has many obstructions, take some measurements early in your planning to make sure the project is feasible.

Local codes specify the minimum sizes for specific rooms. The chart on the opposite page summarizes typical requirements listed by HUD as well as many local codes. (Be sure to consult your own building code.) The chart includes a sample room size that qualifies for the minimum, as well as a preferred size that would make the room more livable. The minimum sizes are quite small. Whenever possible, design larger rooms. Where figures are omitted there is usually no minimum requirement.

Enlarging the floor area. If the basement is not large enough and it occupies only a small portion of the space under your home, you may be able to enlarge it. The customary technique is to dig out space under the house. To avoid undermining the existing foundation, stop the new excavation 2 or 3 feet short of the foundation. The new basement walls then help to retain the soil supporting the foundation. The resulting space has less potential window area than normal basements, but it can be useful as storage space, a wine cellar, a cozy alcove, or a recreation room.

Although excavating dirt is a cheap way to gain new living space, the costs of such a project can go up quickly if water or sewage pipes, a septic tank, or other utility lines are in the way. It is also not very cost-effective if you are adding only a small amount of space. Concrete retaining walls higher than 3 feet are complicated, and codes often demand that they be designed by an engineer. The cost of enlarging a basement may be prohibitive to gain only a few extra square feet, but worthwhile for a large space. Seek the advice of an architect, structural engineer, or general contractor experienced in basement work.

Is the structure stable?

Basement walls and floor should be sound. There should be no major cracks or evidence of settling or other structural problems. Survey the walls and floor yourself to get a general idea of the soundness. If you find any of the following conditions, seek the advice of an architect, engineer, or foundation contractor for further diagnosis. If none of these problems exist, and the walls, floor, and ceiling are level and plumb, you can proceed with your plans.

Problems to look for
☐ Cracks wider than ¼ inch.
☐ Cracks that ''move'' over a few weeks of observation. Draw a dark line across the crack and check it weekly to see if there is movement.
☐ Sunken or buckled floor areas.
☐ Walls that are not vertical.
☐ Excessive moisture.
☐ Separation of wood floor framing from the top of the foundation wall.
☐ Sagging in any floor joists or other framing members.
☐ Wood posts with rot at the bottom.

Enlarging a basement

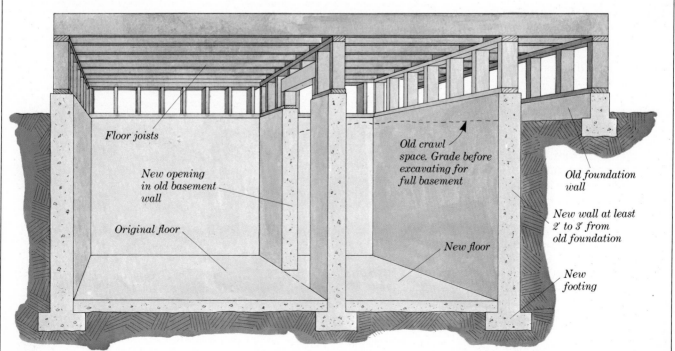

Floor joists

New opening in old basement wall

Original floor

Old crawl space. Grade before excavating for full basement

Old foundation wall

New wall at least 2' to 3' from old foundation

New floor

New footing

Is the basement dry?

Moisture can be a major problem in a basement. It causes dampness, odors, mildew, puddles, insect invasions, and even structural damage. All moisture problems should be taken care of several months, or at least a couple of seasons, before a basement is converted into living space. Make sure that the repairs have worked before proceeding with your plans.

Moisture problems

To stop moisture effectively, you must find the source of the problem. A great deal of money and effort can be wasted by treating only the symptoms and not the main problem.

Moisture comes either from inside the basement (condensation) or from outside (seepage or leaks). Leaks are easy to detect and are caused by a problem outside. The effects of condensation and seepage are similar, but you must differentiate between them because the cures are different.

Condensation is caused by cool surfaces collecting moisture from warm air. If the basement is damp or musty only during hot weather, or if water forms on cold water pipes as readily as the walls (sweating), most likely the cause is condensation. A simple test is to tape a piece of plastic sheeting to the wall and leave it up for a few days. If water forms on the outer surface but the wall under the plastic stays dry, the problem is condensation. If moisture forms under the plastic, then the problem is seepage. Repeat the test after a few weeks to be absolutely sure.

Curing condensation. Normal construction techniques for finishing a basement go a long way toward preventing condensation. Wall insulation, with a vapor barrier over it, prevents warm basement air from contacting the cool masonry walls, which is the cause of most condensation. Exposed pipes and other cold surfaces should also be insulated.

Additional windows will increase air circulation and help prevent condensation. If this is not enough, increasing the movement of air with cross-ventilation or a fan will help. In extreme cases a dehumidifier may be necessary.

Curing seepage. The most likely causes of seepage are faulty downspouts and improper grading around the house. Inspect the roof gutters and downspouts for leaks and fix them. Make sure runoff from the downspouts is carried at least 8 feet away from the house. Soil should be graded away from the house for at least 6 feet, sloped at a rate of at least ½ inch per foot.

If these problems are fixed and water still seeps into the basement, the cause may be a leaking water pipe, sewer pipe, or a line from a central air-conditioning unit.

To check for leaks in a sprinkler system, turn off the main valve for a few days and see if the basement leak dries up. To check for leaks in the main water-supply pipe, turn off the valve at the meter when you leave on a short vacation; inspect the basement when you return. Leakage from a broken sewer pipe will cause an obvious odor, but you can also check by putting a dye, such as food coloring, in the toilet tank and flushing the toilet. If any of these tests indicate a plumbing leak, the only solution is to dig up the pipe and replace it.

Curing severe moisture problems. Persistent leaking, puddles, or flooding are major problems that are difficult to solve. They can sometimes be fixed by waterproofing the interior walls and sealing all the cracks and joints with hydraulic cement. However, a more reliable method is to waterproof the outside of the walls and install drain lines. This works well when the house is on sloping ground. Sometimes a diversion drain, installed upslope from the house, is all that is needed.

If the house is on level ground, the problem is likely to be a high water table. This is the most difficult moisture problem of all. The water exerts continuous pressure against the lower walls and floor and can even cause the floor to buckle and crack. The only recourse is to install a sump pump and forget about using the basement as finished space.

Sometimes it is possible to keep the basement dry by installing drainage pipes around the outside of the foundation, running them into a deep well in the backyard, and installing a sump pump in the well. For these problems, consult with a soils engineer or a contractor specializing in drainage systems.

Severe moisture problems

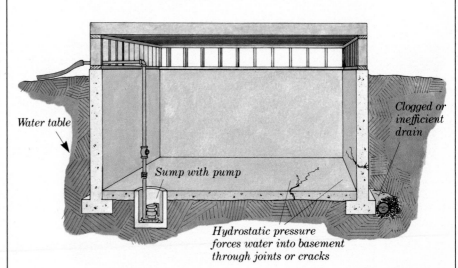

Water table

Clogged or inefficient drain

Sump with pump

Hydrostatic pressure forces water into basement through joints or cracks

Is there enough daylight?

Basement windows are few and small, so one of your first design goals is to add windows and brighten up the space with as much daylight as possible. Almost any type of window can be used in a basement, but metal-framed ones are a good choice because they withstand dampness.

Add large windows. Any wall substantially above grade (the downslope wall of a hillside home, for example) is a possible window location. Bring in more light with large windows that extend down as far as possible or with glass doors. Avoid placing all the windows on just one wall. Doing this may result in a cavelike atmosphere with harsh glare and deep shadows.

Cluster small windows. If your basement does not have a wall in which large windows can be installed easily, cluster several small windows in one area. The windows can all be the same size as existing basement windows and as close together as is structurally possible.

Create a large window well. If it is impossible to add new windows, concentrate on enlarging only one—in a grand manner. Change it to a picture window by excavating a larger window well. Then create a garden in the well with terraced retaining walls, cascading plants, even a waterfall. Add outdoor lighting, and you will have a dramatic focal point both at night and during the day.

This type of well could even serve as an entrance to the basement if it is deep enough for a door. Add patio paving, stairs, a floor drain, and a railing to keep toddlers from falling into the well.

Window placement

In a basement, where daylight is naturally limited, it is important to make the most of each window. When choosing new window locations or planning rooms around existing windows, consider the following factors.

Orientation. Direct sunlight, especially during winter months, is a bonus in any basement. Windows facing south will give you winter sunlight at midday as long as the sun is not blocked by hills, buildings, or trees. If you enjoy a room filled with morning sunlight, take advantage of east-facing windows. West-facing windows are the most likely to cause overheating during summer months. If a window faces north, you will get little direct sunlight (other than on early summer mornings) but you can get bright light from reflected sunlight off a nearby, light-colored wall.

Views. Take advantage of pleasant views, even if it means changing room arrangements around. You can conceal undesirable views with glass blocks, obscure glass, opaque curtains, or shoji screens.

Size of light well. You can bring in more light by enlarging the size of the well. This also makes the view more appealing and dispels any feeling of being closed in.

Privacy and noise. If privacy is important, avoid placing basement windows close to a sidewalk or a neighboring house. If the problem is unavoidable, use fences, walls, and plantings to maintain privacy.

If windows for a quiet room face the street or other noisy area, consider double-glazed windows. Plan a sound barrier, such as a low masonry wall or solid fence, to protect you from noise when the windows are open. The barrier must extend all the way to the ground and should have no openings.

Skylights. If there is just no way to install windows, consider capturing daylight by cutting an opening into the basement ceiling to let in light from the room above. Doing this will cut into the upstairs floor area, but it may be worthwhile if it makes the entire basement usable.

Letting in light

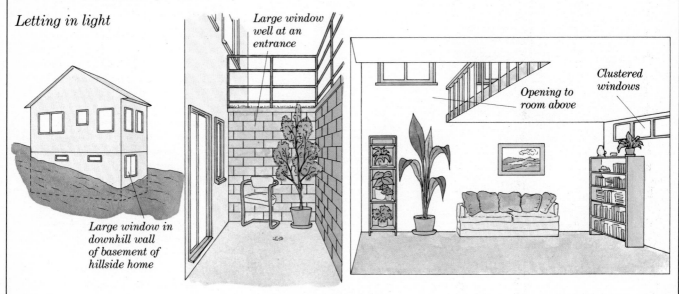

Large window in downhill wall of basement of hillside home

Large window well at an entrance

Opening to room above

Clustered windows

Is there adequate access?

Access to the basement is a major design issue that should be considered early in your planning. Stairs may need to be changed or moved to make them safe, inviting, and convenient; this will affect other design decisions. In addition, codes require that some rooms, such as bedrooms, have direct egress to the outside, through a window or a separate door.

Code requirements

Most codes distinguish between primary and secondary stairs. Stairs to unfinished basements are usually considered secondary stairs, which have less stringent code requirements than main stairs between living spaces. However, when a basement is converted to living space, the stairs may have to meet the primary-stair code requirements. Even if your local code allows secondary stairs (some do when the living space is less than 400 square feet), it is a good idea to upgrade them for safety reasons.

The following dimensions are the typical code requirements for primary stairs:
7½-inch maximum riser height
9-inch minimum tread depth
32-inch minimum stair width between handrails
80-inch minimum headroom
30- to 33-inch handrail height
36-inch-deep platform

Other requirements may include installing a second handrail if the stairs are wider than 4 feet; conforming to a minimum width of winders; and installing a landing if an access door swings over the stairs.

If the existing stairs are not adequate for primary stairs, consider:
☐ Rebuilding the stairs in the same location.
☐ Building new stairs in a different location and either removing the existing stairs or leaving them to be used as secondary access.
☐ Building a new exterior entry as the primary access. This involves breaching the foundation wall, excavating a stairwell on the outside of the wall, and building the stairs.

How will the space be heated?

Heating a basement is not difficult. If the house has a central heating system with the furnace in the basement, the furnace itself may generate sufficient heat. If not, there will be ducts close at hand that you can tap into to install new registers. If the house has a hydronic (hot water) system, it should be easy to extend the pipes into the basement. Electric baseboard units or small gas appliances can also be installed. Remember that gas heaters must be vented.

Fireplace or wood stove. Although it may not qualify as the primary heat source, a fireplace or wood-burning stove adds great appeal to a basement. It must be located where a chimney can be run either up through unused space in the house or up an exterior wall. Use only chimney pipe approved by local codes and maintain minimum clearances between the pipe and any combustible materials such as wood. The typical requirements are 2 inches for framing members, 1 inch for all others. A new stove cannot be vented into an existing flue if any other heaters are already vented into it.

How will the space be cooled?

In most climates, keeping the main house cool will usually keep a basement cool as long as air circulates freely. Cross-ventilation between open windows helps, although it may only move the air near the ceiling. One way to move the lower air is to build a baffle or shield against one window; it should extend almost to the floor. This allows the air near the floor to go up and out of that window but it will only work when there is incoming air from the opposite window to create a flow across the room.

You can also use fans and, if necessary, air conditioning to keep a basement cool in extremely hot climates.

Safer basement access

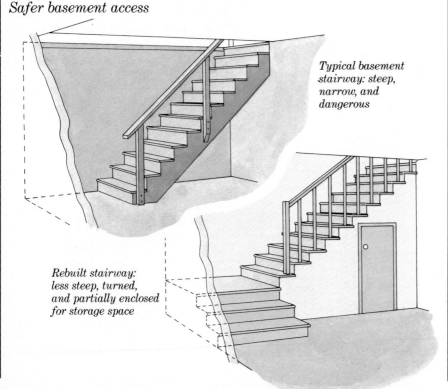

Typical basement stairway: steep, narrow, and dangerous

Rebuilt stairway: less steep, turned, and partially enclosed for storage space

How should the space be insulated?

Requirements for insulating a basement vary widely, depending on climate. Your building department will specify what is required in your area.

Upper wall. The most critical section for basement insulation is the upper wall between the frostline and first-floor walls, particularly along the rim joist. If a basement ceiling is already in place, remove it to gain access to the rim joist area and install fiberglass blanket insulation. The rest of the upper wall can be insulated on the outside with rigid foam boards, although this is not necessary if you are insulating the entire inside wall.

Lower wall. Although the earth provides some insulation for the lower parts of a basement wall, in most areas it is advisable to insulate the entire wall.

Installing insulation. There are two ways to insulate basement walls. The first is to glue rigid foam panels to the foundation walls between vertical wood furring strips. The second is to install fiberglass blankets between conventional studs.

In either case the insulation should be covered by ½-inch wallboard. The type you use depends on whether you need to build a conventional stud wall against the masonry foundation walls. This may be necessary if the walls are too irregular to attach a finish wall directly to them.

If you live in a hot climate, it may be inadvisable to insulate at all. By absorbing the heat, the insulation will inhibit the cooling of masonry walls. Get advice from local architects, builders, or cooling specialists.

Insulating the floor. In extremely cold climates the basement floor should also be insulated. The most effective way (impossible in an existing basement) is to place rigid insulating boards under the concrete floor before it is poured. Compromise by installing a wood floor over the concrete and placing rigid insulating boards between the sleepers.

Are there obstructions?

Posts, walls, pipes, utility equipment, and ducts hanging from the ceiling create obstacles in a basement. Most of them are vital parts of the mechanical systems or structure of your home. As moving them tends to be complicated and expensive, try to design the basement space around them.

Pipes and ducts. One way to deal with an obstacle is to conceal it in a wall, ceiling, or freestanding storage unit. If there is enough headroom, you may be able to conceal overhead obstacles in a suspended ceiling. If not, they can be enclosed in a low soffit (providing there is 80 inches of clearance below) or a wall.

Large equipment or clusters of pipes and ducts can be concealed in a separate closet.

Posts. If you are planning a large, open area, you may have to deal with posts. Moving them is a major structural change that should not be considered without getting professional advice. Less drastic solutions include designing a countertop or built-in seating that wraps around the post, boxing in the post with simple framing and wallboard to disguise it as a column, or leaving the post exposed and painting it a bright color.

Obstructions

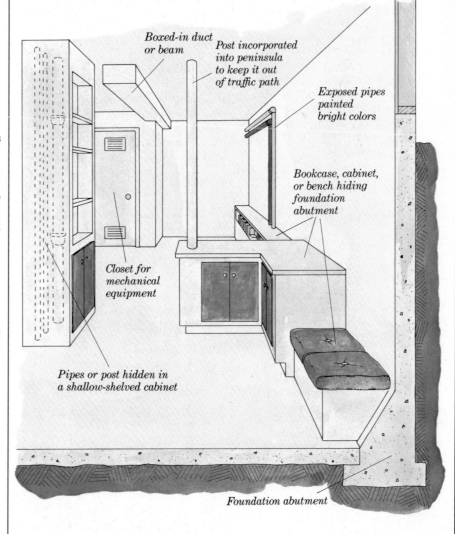

Boxed-in duct or beam

Post incorporated into peninsula to keep it out of traffic path

Exposed pipes painted bright colors

Bookcase, cabinet, or bench hiding foundation abutment

Closet for mechanical equipment

Pipes or post hidden in a shallow-shelved cabinet

Foundation abutment

Are plumbing hookups possible?

Before you plan a bathroom, laundry, or sink for the basement, determine how much plumbing work will be necessary. Although you should consult with an architect or plumber, you can use the following tips for preliminary planning.

Existing fixtures. If there are existing fixtures in the basement, there is a good chance that you can leave them intact, upgrade them, or install new fixtures elsewhere. First determine if the existing fixture is connected to a proper sanitary drain system. If it is a toilet, the drain system is most likely adequate. However, a laundry tub, sink, or other "gray water" fixture may drain into a floor drain or sump. This condition should not be continued and you should proceed as if installing new fixtures.

Existing drain lines. If there are no fixtures in the basement or if the ones that exist are not connected directly to proper drains, look for the main house drain. This is usually a 3- or 4-inch-diameter pipe suspended below the basement ceiling. When you find it, follow its downward path. If it disappears through the basement floor, you can tie new fixture drains into it.

If the main drain disappears through the basement wall instead of the floor, it may not be low enough to tie in new fixtures. If it is just a few inches from the floor, you can build a platform so that the outlets of a toilet, bathtub, or shower are above the main drain.

If the main drain is more than a few inches higher than the floor, you may still be able to connect certain fixtures. A sink drain can be up to 16 to 20 inches off the floor; a washing machine drain can be 18 inches off the floor. Again, a raised platform may enable you to meet these requirements, as long as there is enough headroom.

Installing drain lines. If the main house drain is too high to connect basement fixtures directly to it, there are two other options. One is to install an ejector system. The expense of such a system may be worthwhile if it enables you to install a bathroom.

Individual upflush fixtures are also available, but make sure that your local codes allow them.

The second option is to install a new branch drain under the basement floor and run it into the main house sewer outside the foundation walls. This is possible only if the main sewer is buried lower than the level of the basement floor. It will take a lot of digging, but that may be worthwhile if you have to excavate around the basement walls anyway in order to cure seepage problems.

Plumbing vents. All plumbing fixtures must be vented to the roof. If fixtures already exist, you can use the same vents. If there are no fixtures, you need to run new vent pipes up through the house and attic. The easiest runs are through closets.

Vents can be run through interior walls, but be prepared to hit problem obstructions such as wiring or fireblocks. Exterior walls pose even more of a problem because of windows and insulation. Some codes allow vents to be installed on the outside of the house. This is an easy run even though it will not be attractive.

Plumbing

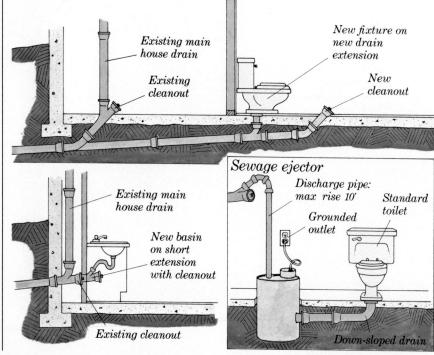

Existing main house drain

Existing cleanout

New fixture on new drain extension

New cleanout

Existing main house drain

New basin on short extension with cleanout

Existing cleanout

Sewage ejector

Discharge pipe: max rise 10'

Standard toilet

Grounded outlet

Down-sloped drain

New vent options

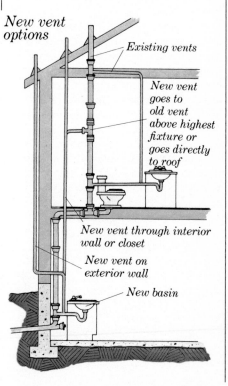

Existing vents

New vent goes to old vent above highest fixture or goes directly to roof

New vent through interior wall or closet

New vent on exterior wall

New basin

What wiring is necessary?

Any new living space requires additional wiring. It may be necessary to upgrade the main system to accommodate new basement wiring, but the actual arrangement of the basement space will not be affected by wiring requirements. New wiring can be planned around the space but must meet code-required safety and convenience needs. If you prefer, you can plan the wiring after the final design is complete.

Install basement wiring as you would in any other room unless you are dealing with masonry walls. If you are furring out new stud walls from the foundation walls, install the boxes and wiring in the wood framing. If you are leaving the foundation walls bare, mount surface receptacles to the walls with concrete fasteners and run the wiring through conduit.

GFCI protection. Basement wiring requirements are no different from other rooms except that you may be required to have GFCI (ground fault circuit interrupter) protection on receptacles. Codes require this type of protection for outdoor receptacles and in bathrooms, garages, and basements to protect against possible electric shock.

The GFCI devices monitor the current going to the outlets and shut them off instantly whenever there is any danger of shock. The outlet stays dead until the GFCI device is reset. This can cause problems when refrigerators, freezers, computers, and entertainment equipment are plugged into this type of outlet. If you plan to install any such equipment in the basement, hire an electrician to advise you on the best way to ensure reliability as well as safety.

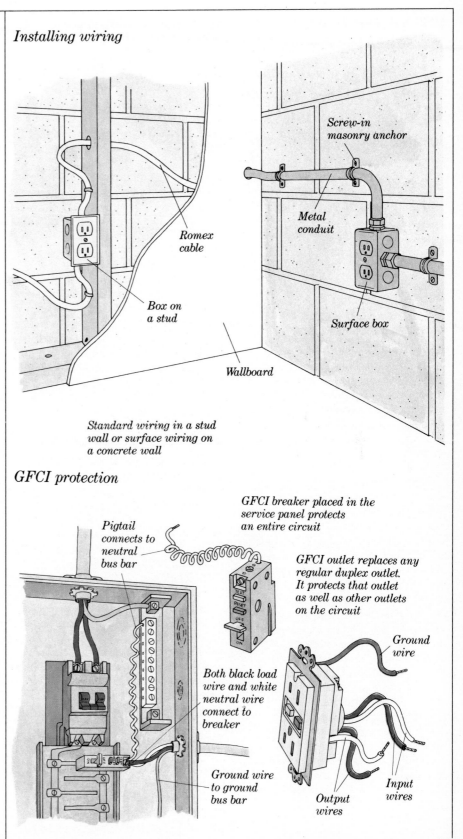

Installing wiring

Screw-in masonry anchor

Metal conduit

Romex cable

Surface box

Box on a stud

Wallboard

Standard wiring in a stud wall or surface wiring on a concrete wall

GFCI protection

Pigtail connects to neutral bus bar

GFCI breaker placed in the service panel protects an entire circuit

GFCI outlet replaces any regular duplex outlet. It protects that outlet as well as other outlets on the circuit

Both black load wire and white neutral wire connect to breaker

Ground wire to ground bus bar

Ground wire

Input wires

Output wires

MAKING THE SPACE APPEALING

The elements that will contribute to the appeal of your basement include finished surfaces, trim, lighting, storage, and special features. These add drama or interest, even though they may not solve any particular design problems.

Good design is the successful integration of all components—structural, functional, and decorative—not just the addition of a few special features.

Finishing the floor

A concrete floor can be carpeted, tiled, covered with wood or resilient flooring, or just painted. If there is a slight moisture problem, tile, resilient flooring, or nonorganic carpet materials will not be harmed by a small amount of moisture wicking up through the concrete.

Carpet is a good choice for basements because it is soft, resilient, quiet, and warm. It also hides surface irregularities well.

Tile and resilient sheet materials are good choices for rooms where maintenance and durability are primary concerns. Tile is cool to the touch, which may be an advantage in hot climates. Resilient materials are softer and are offered in a great variety of colors and patterns.

Wood floors can be installed directly over concrete or, for more resilience, on a wooden subfloor. But wood will be damaged if there is a moisture problem. Consult with a flooring specialist before choosing a wood floor for a basement.

Install flooring materials directly over the concrete or over a wood subfloor for a more resilient surface.

Finishing the walls

In some cases the original foundation walls may be adequate for finish walls, particularly if they are brick or stone. If they are dry and you are not installing insulation, you can just paint them. If they are concrete or concrete block, you can dress them up with stone or brick veneer.

A more common treatment for walls is to finish them with wallboard. This makes it possible to add insulation and makes basement space look more like conventional rooms. Wallboard can be painted, paneled, or covered with wallcoverings.

Wall treatments add to the comfort of a basement. Paneling has long been a favorite material for warming up a space, although it can also make it feel dark and cramped if overdone. If you do install paneling, first apply wallboard over the insulation for fire protection. Always be sure moisture problems are corrected before you finish any walls.

Finishing a low ceiling

Basement ceilings are a challenge to finish because they are low and often interrupted by ducts and pipes. If there is at least 90 inches of headroom, conceal all the ducts with a continuous suspended ceiling. If not, box them in (as long as there is at least 80 inches of clearance) or leave them exposed and paint them.

To overcome an oppressive feeling, make the ceiling lower where it abuts the walls. This stepped-down section will make the center part of the ceiling appear higher than it is. Applying coving all around the edges will give a similar effect.

Light colors tend to heighten a ceiling; dark colors lower it. The safest approach is white paint. An alternative is to use the same hue in graduating intensities. Start with the darkest shades around the edges and proceed with lighter tints toward the center, carefully blending them together. The result is exciting and

dramatic, but like all illusions it must be handled skillfully.

Another dramatic effect is to paint the ceiling flat black and nail on wood lattice, stained or painted a light color. This gives the appearance of a canopy, rather than a low ceiling.

Rather than trying to disguise the cavelike atmosphere, you can exploit it by creating a cozy getaway where windows and high ceilings will never be missed. Darken the ceiling, cover the walls with brick or stone veneer, install a fireplace, cover the floor with soft carpeting, and add built-in seating platforms.

Techniques for enlarging space

Even if a basement has ample floor area, the following techniques will make a low ceiling appear higher.

☐ Use small-scale, light-colored furnishings clustered in groups rather than scattered around. A clean, well-organized space dispels uneasiness caused by a low ceiling.

☐ Install wall-mounted or ceiling fixtures instead of floor lamps.

☐ Lay continuous floor covering in a light, neutral color instead of scatter rugs to unify and simplify the space.

☐ Cover a wall with large mirrors, especially a long wall in a narrow space. It will make the room feel wider and will divert attention away from the low ceiling.

☐ Install curved walls rather than right-angled corners. This will create the illusion of more open space and will make room dimensions, including height, less predictable.

☐ Accentuate vertical lines to make walls appear taller. Stopping paneling short of the ceiling will also make the ceiling seem higher.

☐ Build room dividers instead of walls where noise or privacy are not important. Seeing over the tops of dividers will make the ceiling feel higher.

Eastern touches blended with Western furnishings result in a sophisticated basement spa. Shoji screens can be pulled across to separate the large soaking tub from the conversation area.

Choosing finish details

The final design will include specifications for trim materials, moldings, doors, lighting fixtures, hardware items, window coverings, plumbing fixtures, and other finish details.

It is easy to put off these decisions until the space is actually under construction, and many people do. Often the architect specifies "furnished by owner" for some of the details in the plans, or an allowance is included in the contractor's bid package for items not specified. This approach is valid, but you should try to finalize all these details during the design phase, even if you make changes later on.

For one thing, these features represent a significant part of the budget. Considering them in the early planning stages minimizes the chances of overlooking expensive items, and gives you time to research and evaluate available options. Some choices may affect other design issues. You will also have the benefit of professional advice when the plans are still being formed and your architect and designer are thinking most critically about the details. Finally, knowing that every detail of the plan is settled before the bidding and construction begin frees you to focus on—even anticipate—problems and issues rather than having the project languish because a decision has not been made or a key item procured.

Choosing fixtures for a basement is no different from choosing them for other rooms. Decisions will depend on functional needs, cost, suitability, and individual preference.

Eyesores such as pipes and ducts become almost invisible when painted a dark color and covered by a suspended lattice ceiling. In this basement, redwood built-ins provide ample storage space for a serious wine cellar.

Planning lighting

A good lighting system enhances any room, but in a basement it is a particularly important part of the design. Use lighting to accent desirable features and downplay drawbacks.

As with any lighting design, basement lighting should include general illumination for safety and convenience. You can best achieve this with indirect fixtures that cast a warm glow over large areas, such as a globe, or directional fixtures such as sconces that wash a wall with light.

Task lighting is needed for specific work or reading areas. It is usually focused on counters, desks, reading areas, or work tables, by using table lamps or suspended ceiling fixtures.

Accent lighting provides the decoration. It is usually aimed at specific objects or architectural features, by means of spotlights, wall sconces, or recessed canisters.

Use the following techniques to make a basement ceiling appear higher and the effect more exciting.
☐ Place lights on the floor and direct them upward against a wall (up-lighting) to heighten it.
☐ Use wall sconces to accentuate the walls instead of the low ceiling.
☐ Place valances near the ceiling, but direct the light downward to divert attention away from the ceiling.
☐ Use recessed ceiling lights to provide sufficient general illumination from a hidden source.
☐ Install dimmer switches for lights.

Planning a lighting system is much more than choosing a fixture for the middle of your ceiling. It is the creation of a total environment. An interior designer, architect, or lighting specialist can help you design a lighting plan that may be the most exciting element of your new basement.

Planning storage

A good basement design includes plenty of storage, both for basement activities and for extra household goods. Chances are that your unfinished basement is already a prime storage area for your home, so you will want to set aside a certain amount of space for the same purpose. Consider these storage ideas.
☐ Plan a separate storage room.
☐ Put "dead" space to work for storage. The area under stairs, odd corners around furnace equipment, and shallow crawl space under other parts of the house are good possibilities.
☐ Install floor-to-ceiling shelves or storage units wherever possible.
☐ Cover an entire wall with storage units. Wide cabinets on the bottom and open shelves on top make a long countertop possible.
☐ Use the space underneath windows set high on a wall.
☐ Fill the ceiling space above doorways, the area around fireplaces, and any other nooks and crannies with shelves and storage units.
☐ Organize closets with dividers and shelf units for maximum efficiency.
☐ Buy or build platform beds with built-in storage units.
☐ Build benches with storage below, instead of using chairs.

Adding built-in seating

Built-in benches or sofas (banquettes) offer many advantages. They can be built to fit room dimensions and, if wide enough, can double as beds for overnight guests. Having built-ins allows you to clear space in the center of the room for recreational purposes. They provide useful storage for items you do not want on view and make good use of awkward wall space under high basement windows.

Adding an outside entrance

An outside entrance provides emergency egress and solves practical problems such as moving in large fixtures and appliances.

Although any entrance is better than none, try to plan one that admits as much natural light as possible. Use glass doors. (If security is a problem, this approach is not advisable.) Plan a well large enough to lay a small patio at the foot of the stairs. Slope or terrace the sides of the well so that more sky will be visible and to afford the opportunity to create a garden.

Try to provide an entrance with a transition between outdoors and indoors: Cover the opening with a porch or a prefabricated greenhouse.

Adding a bathroom

A bathroom will be essential if you plan to convert a basement into a separate apartment, a master bedroom suite, or a guest room. But it is also a welcome convenience in any type of conversion. Even a tiny powder room is more convenient than trudging up and down stairs. And the cost and effort involved in squeezing a bathroom into your basement is normally offset by the increased value of your home.

Including a fireplace or wood stove

Nothing adds coziness and warmth to a space as much as a fireplace or wood-burning stove. It is especially effective in basements because an underground space can feel cold and uninviting, and because basements have plenty of wall space. A fireplace also creates a strong focal point, which basements often lack since they rarely have dramatic windows or other interesting features.

The most practical type of fireplace to install in an existing room is a zeroclearance model. This has an insulated metal enclosure and a chimney that can be boxed in with ordinary wood framing and wallboard. Many models have glass doors and other energy-saving features.

Wood-burning stoves are more energy efficient than fireplaces, take up less room, and may be simple to install if the concrete floor and masonry walls are exposed.

Chimneys. Finding a place to run the chimney for either a fireplace or a wood-burning stove may be the biggest design problem. The easiest method is to run an approved metal chimney up from the fireplace or stove, out through the top of the basement wall, and up the exterior wall of the house. It can then be boxed in to match the siding.

You may already have a brick or masonry chimney in the basement but, if it serves an upstairs fireplace or stove, it is illegal to hook another appliance to it. If the existing chimney is no longer used, you may be able to use it as long as the upstairs flue openings are sealed up. Check with your local building department for specific regulations, and hire a chimney sweep or fireplace specialist to do a thorough inspection before you consider hooking up a new appliance to an existing chimney.

Making stairs more attractive

Do not overlook the stairway when you consider ways to make your basement more appealing. A stairway can be the focal point of your whole design. For a dramatic design element, consider opening up the basement ceiling around the stairway. This will add space, daylight, and an interesting overlook from above. Or install a wide, curved stairway instead of a standard, straight-run design.

If these techniques are too bold for your tastes or too much for your budget, there are many ways to dress up a more conventional stairway.

☐ Cover the treads with either hardwood or carpeting.

☐ Replace the overhead light with several low lights.

☐ Use a tubular handrail in brightly colored plastic or metal.

☐ Add a bend in the stairway toward the bottom for interest and variety.

☐ Cut openings in one wall of the stairwell to admit light and to catch glimpses of the basement room as you descend.

☐ Replace the door at the top of the stairs with a French door.

☐ Dress up a bare wall at the end with a mirror, wall hanging, painting, sculpture, or plant display.

A porthole window and a secretary provide points of interest and make the area at the foot of the stairs a usable space. Wood-paneled walls add to the feeling that this is a functional room rather than merely a landing.

O*nce the design is finished and plans have been approved for a permit, you are ready to begin the construction process.*

Some of the work in a basement conversion is similar to any other type of home-improvment project: plumbing, wiring, wallboard, finish work, flooring, painting. For techniques and more information about these skills, refer to *Ortho's Home Improvement Encyclopedia* or books on specific home-improvement projects.

Whether you hire a contractor to do all the construction or do some or all of the work yourself, there are some general principles of basement construction that are helpful to keep in mind.

☐ If new or rebuilt stairs are required, rough them in as soon as possible. Add the hardwood for the treads or lay the carpeting only at the end of the project.

☐ If you are installing a large window, delay closing up the opening until most of the work is completed. Use the opening for access during construction.

☐ If there is no door at the top of a stairwell, seal the opening with a tarp or plastic sheeting to control dust.

Preventing moisture problems

A basement should be completely dry before you convert it into living space. Although basement moisture problems are common, they are not inevitable if a basement is built properly in the first place. You cannot rebuild your basement to solve moisture problems, but you may be able to make some improvements. It will be helpful to review the following techniques used in new construction to ensure a dry basement.

☐ Install a waterproof membrane underneath the basement floor.

☐ Apply a thick coat of water-proofing material on the outside of the foundation walls.

☐ Lay drainage pipes near the footing to collect subsurface water and discharge it far from the house.

☐ Place crushed rock or plastic drain mats against the wall to divert water down to the pipe.

☐ Compact backfill around the drain rock or drain mat.

☐ Extend downspouts to divert runoff water from the roof at least 10 feet away from the house.

☐ Grade the soil around the house so it slopes away for at least 6 feet, ½ inch per foot.

All these techniques are preventive measures: They keep water from reaching the basement walls and floor. Preventive measures are also the best way to cure moisture problems in an existing basement, although superficial dampproofing,

such as coating the inside surface of the floor and walls with a sealing agent, may be enough in some cases. The first step is to find out where the moisture comes from.

Diagnosing and curing water problems

With some detective work you should be able to find the exact cause of basement moisture problems, although the process may take a few weeks, or even several months. Following are remedies for some of the most likely culprits.

Surface water. If the grading around the house does not slope away properly, water can collect near the foundation. It eventually seeps into the basement, most noticeably after rainstorms. This problem can develop suddenly due to settlement of the soil, especially in homes 40 to 50 years old. Walks and patios next to

Deflecting water

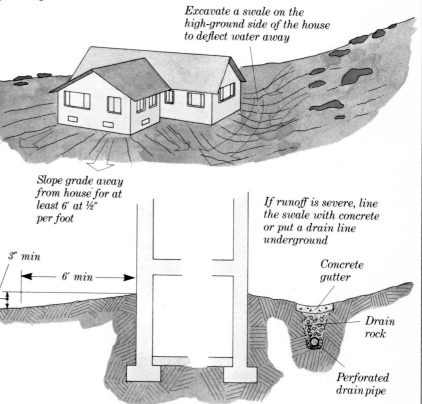

Excavate a swale on the high-ground side of the house to deflect water away

Slope grade away from house for at least 6' at ½" per foot

3" min

6' min

If runoff is severe, line the swale with concrete or put a drain line underground

Concrete gutter

Drain rock

Perforated drain pipe

the house may also settle over time and slope toward the foundation.

The remedy for this problem is to regrade the soil around the house. It may require a small bulldozer, which you can rent if you want to do the work yourself. Where high ground surrounds part of your home, excavate a shallow depression, or swale, to create proper slope away from the house. It should drain easily to lower ground (as long as it is not the neighbors' property). If surface runoff is severe, line the bottom of the swale with a concrete gutter to minimize ground saturation, or bury a drain line under the center of the swale.

A concrete patio or walk is more difficult to regrade. You can reslope the surface with a special patching compound if the original concrete is sound and you paint or seal the patching material to prevent a freeze-thaw cycle from lifting it off. If the concrete is cracked from settling, which is likely, the best remedy is to remove or replace it.

Roof runoff. Gutters and downspouts should not leak or get blocked by trapped debris. Even if they are in good condition, the water discharged from the downspouts can still seep into the basement unless it is carried at least 8 feet away from the house.

There are two ways to lead the water away from the downspout. You can use surface conduits, such as plastic pipe, a long splash block, or a flexible perforated tube to disperse the water. Alternatively you can install underground drainpipes to carry the water to a city storm sewer, a drywell dug in the yard, or to low ground away from the house.

If the downspouts are already connected to underground drainpipes, do not assume everything is taken care of. The drainpipes may be clogged or misaligned, causing water to back up and saturate the ground near the house. To check, observe joints in the downspouts during a rainstorm to see if water backs up, or test with a hose during dry weather. If drainpipes are clogged, clear them with a drain auger or replace them.

Window wells. A window well collects water, which will seep into the ground next to the house if it is not carried off. The most effective drainage system is a concrete floor with a drain that carries water away from the house. If the well does not have a concrete floor, you can dig a trench around the outside to a depth lower than the floor, install 4-inch-diameter drainpipe, cover the pipe with drain rock, and backfill. The drainpipe should terminate in a drywell, storm sewer, or low land.

Subsurface water. If treatments for surface runoff do not cure basement moisture problems, the cause may be permanent underground water. A high water table is a serious threat to basements, and you will need professional help to deal with it. The common procedure is to dig a trench around the foundation, waterproof the walls from the outside, install a 4-inch-diameter drainpipe at the footing, cover it with drain rock, and backfill. This is an expensive cure and may not work if the water table forces water up through the floor.

Underground water does not always come from a high water table. It may be seepage from higher ground, running just a few feet below the surface. If so, a simple flashing system installed in the ground may be enough to divert the water away from the basement. Dig a shallow trench along the entire length of the problem wall, 2 to 3 feet deep and 3 to 4 feet wide. Lay a sheet of 6-mil plastic or special waterproofing membrane in the trench, lapping the edge up the wall and attaching it with roof mastic or caulking. Fill in the trench, sloping the backfill away from the house at the surface.

Drainage

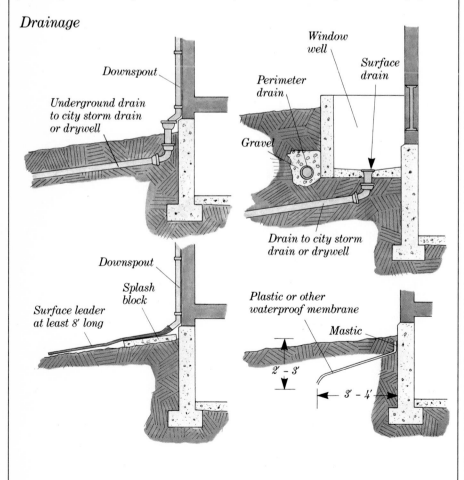

Downspout

Underground drain to city storm drain or drywell

Window well

Perimeter drain

Surface drain

Gravel

Drain to city storm drain or drywell

Downspout

Splash block

Surface leader at least 8' long

Plastic or other waterproof membrane

Mastic

2' - 3'

3' - 4'

Installing floors

Installing a new concrete floor, whether to gain headroom or to replace a damaged floor, is a major project. You should seek advice from an engineer, builder, or architect who specializes in basements, especially if the project involves any shoring or there are moisture problems. Because most of the work is demolition and excavation, you may want to do it yourself.

If the existing concrete floor is sound, but you would prefer a more resilient surface, you can install a wood subfloor over the concrete. This is a lot easier than installing a new concrete floor.

Lowering a basement floor

Provide temporary shoring to support main floor beams so existing columns or posts can be replaced with longer ones. Place temporary posts on both sides of each column.

Break a hole in the concrete floor at least 2 feet square and dig to 6 inches below the new floor level.

Place a wide timber, thick wood pad, or precast concrete pier on the bottom of the hole.

Place a jack column or post with screw jack or "jack pier" under it, on the pad. Jack the post up until it fits snugly against the beam.

For safety, nail cleats or metal connectors to both the post and beam.

Tighten the jack periodically to counteract compaction of the soil.

Remove old columns.

Remove concrete and excavate. Because of the limited access to basements, this is pick-and-shovel work. For extensive digging, consider renting an electric jackhammer with a pointed bit for concrete and a spade bit for heavy clay, a small bulldozer if your basement has a grade-level entry, and a conveyor belt.

You should also plan ahead of time how you will dispose of the dirt and broken concrete, whether hiring someone to haul it away, hauling it away yourself, or distributing it around your yard.

Outline the limits of the excavation on the old concrete floor. Do not dig closer to walls than 2 feet or you will undermine them.

Break up the old concrete with a sledge hammer or jackhammer and remove it. (Wear gloves, safety goggles, and dust mask.)

Excavate to a depth of 6 inches below the new finish floor.

Build perimeter walls. The low re-taining walls will stabilize the soil supporting the foundation and provide a finish surface for the basement space. If they are above a certain height, usually 3 feet, they must be designed by an engineer.

Excavate a footing trench 12 inches wide and 6 inches deep.

Build vertical forms for a wall 6 inches wide to the height of the original concrete floor.

Place horizontal rebar (#4) at the top and bottom of the wall, at least 3 inches away from the soil and 1½

Lowering the floor

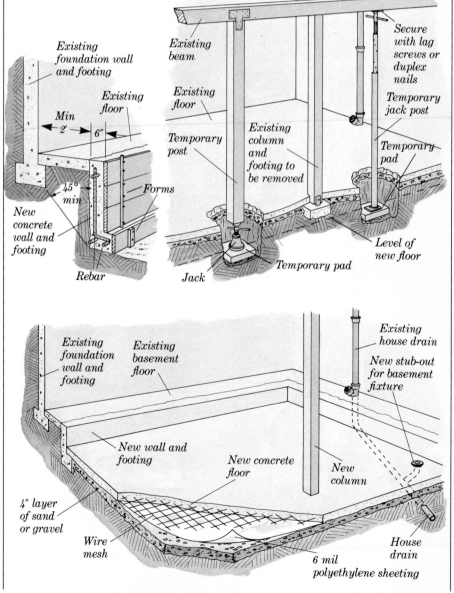

Existing foundation wall and footing

Existing floor

Min 2' 6"

New concrete wall and footing

45° min

Forms

Rebar

Existing beam

Existing floor

Temporary post

Existing column and footing to be removed

Jack

Temporary pad

Secure with lag screws or duplex nails

Temporary jack post

Temporary pad

Level of new floor

Existing foundation wall and footing

Existing basement floor

New wall and footing

New concrete floor

4" layer of sand or gravel

Wire mesh

New column

Existing house drain

New stub-out for basement fixture

House drain

6 mil polyethylene sheeting

inches away from exposed faces.

Place vertical rebar as required, usually 18 inches on center and fill the forms with concrete. Vibrate the concrete, screed it off at the top, and let it cure for five days before removing the forms.

Pour a new concrete floor. Install all underfloor plumbing or drain lines.

Lay 2 to 4 inches of sand or gravel and compact it with a power tamper. Install rigid insulation, if needed.

Using plastic at least 4 mil thick, install a moisture barrier, lapping it 2 to 3 inches up the walls. Overlap any joins in the plastic by about 6 inches.

Place material against the walls for isolation joints, such as rigid insulation, beveled siding boards, or special isolation joint fillers.

Install steel reinforcing mesh; use 2-inch cement blocks (dobies) or wire "chairs" to center it in the concrete. Tie it to any rebar protruding from the wall footings.

Place, vibrate, screed, and finish the concrete to a minimum thickness of 4 inches. Cure by covering with plastic sheeting or spray-on curing compound. (Avoid using compound if you will be adhering tile, vinyl, carpet, or other materials directly to the concrete floor.)

Resurfacing a concrete floor

If the floor is cracked, broken, or damaged, it is possible to resurface it. You can either level the existing floor or you can add a new floor on top of the old one.

Self-leveling underlayment compound. If the floor is sloped and rough, but structurally sound, level it with one of several liquid mortar products available from concrete suppliers or construction materials companies. Simply mix up the compound, pour it onto the floor, and spread it out. It levels itself and hardens to a smooth, water-resistant surface without troweling. If you want it thicker than ½ inch, add aggregate. The surface can also be feathered to blend into the original concrete floor. Always apply compound according to manufacturer's instructions, which usually specify a primer applied at least a day before.

New structural slab. If the floor is not structurally sound and has severe cracks and sunken areas, it may be possible to pour a new concrete slab on top, providing there is enough headroom. First seek professional advice to determine the cause, because problems caused by unstable soils, a high water table, or shifting foundation walls require more elaborate treatments. If no such problems exist, do the following to install a new slab.

Install any new piping or plumbing drains. Add extenders to floor drains. Lay waterproof plastic membrane over the existing floor.

Place special joint fillers or ½-inch rigid insulation for isolation joints around the perimeter.

Place steel reinforcement, such as 6 by 6, #10 wire mesh. Use cement blocks or wire "chairs" to center it in the concrete.

Pour 4 inches of concrete; use the isolation joints for screeding it level. Smooth the surface and cover with polyethylene sheeting to cure.

Liquid mortar underlayment

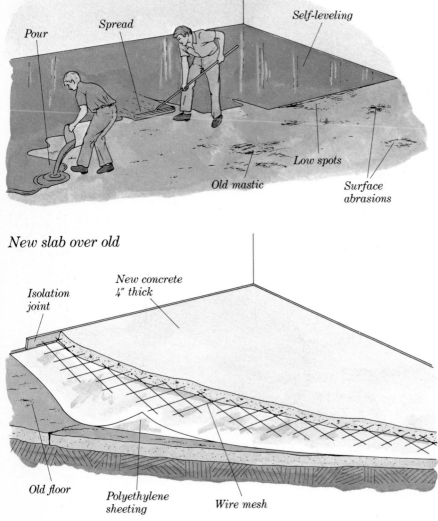

New slab over old

87

Installing a wood subfloor

To create a more resilient surface for installing carpet, resilient tile, sheet vinyl, or wood flooring, use the following procedure for laying down a wood subfloor. It is also a good way to moistureproof a floor subject to mild dampness.

Be sure severe moisture problems are solved. Apply one coat of asphalt emulsion sealer and spread 6-mil polyethylene sheeting over it, overlapping sheets 6 inches. Lap edges up the wall 6 inches; hold with tape.

Use a powder-actuated fastening tool (stud driver) to attach pressure-treated 1 by 3 or 1 by 4 sleepers to the concrete, 16 inches on center. (Follow safety precautions carefully for using the fastening tool.) Space nails 12 to 16 inches apart. Level the sleepers with cedar shims.

If insulation is needed, lay ¾-inch-thick panels of extruded polystyrene between the sleepers. (For thicker insulation use 2 by 4 sleepers.) In very cold climates glue foam panels directly over the asphalt sealer with #11 mastic and install the sleepers over them.

Attach ⅝-inch tongue-and-groove plywood or ¾-inch particle board (underlayment grade) to the sleepers with construction adhesive and 1½-inch ring-shank nails. Leave a ⅛-inch gap between panels and ½ inch around the walls. Trim the plastic vapor barrier flush with the floor.

Alternative method. If you do not have access to a stud driver, set the sleepers in mastic.

Seal the floor with asphalt emulsion and spread a layer of #11 asphalt mastic over it.

Install polyethylene sheeting, as described above.

Install pressure-treated sleepers, 16 inches on center. Use mastic to adhere them to the plastic. Attach plywood subfloor, as above.

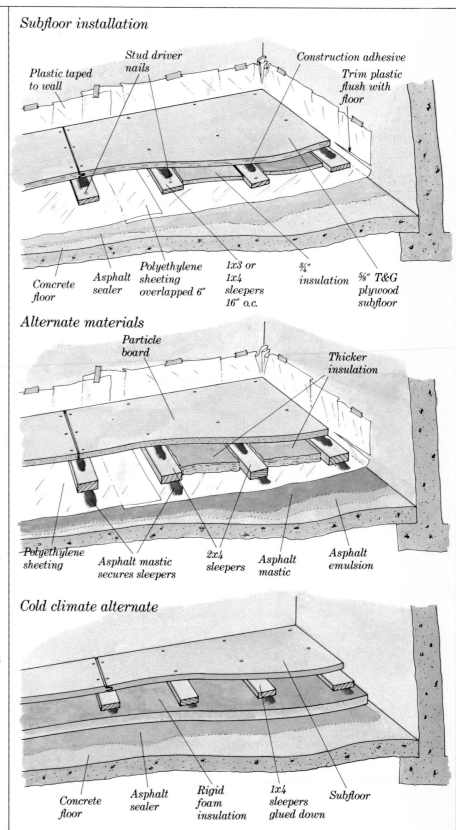

Subfloor installation

Plastic taped to wall • Stud driver nails • Construction adhesive • Trim plastic flush with floor

Concrete floor • Asphalt sealer • Polyethylene sheeting overlapped 6" • 1x3 or 1x4 sleepers 16" o.c. • ¾" insulation • ⅝" T&G plywood subfloor

Alternate materials

Particle board • Thicker insulation

Polyethylene sheeting • Asphalt mastic secures sleepers • 2x4 sleepers • Asphalt mastic • Asphalt emulsion

Cold climate alternate

Concrete floor • Asphalt sealer • Rigid foam insulation • 1x4 sleepers glued down • Subfloor

Installing ceilings

There are different ways to install a basement ceiling, depending on available height and the types of obstructions. If headroom is sufficient, install a continuous suspended ceiling. Otherwise, nail a wallboard ceiling directly to the floor joists, enclosing pipes and ducts in boxes.

The sequence of installing a wall and ceiling depends on the type of ceiling. If it is a suspended ceiling, finish the walls first. If it is a conventional wallboard ceiling attached to the floor joists, install the ceiling before doing the walls.

Installing a suspended ceiling

A suspended ceiling has the advantages of making utility lines accessible, overcoming sagging or uneven joists, making it easier to install light fixtures, and providing sound insulation. Components come in many colors and styles, and instructions for installation are usually included.

Be sure any wall and ceiling areas concealed by the new ceiling are insulated wherever necessary, especially the rim joist area. Insulate any cold water pipes to prevent condensation and dripping problems.

Mark level lines around the walls of the room at the height of the finished ceiling at least 7½ feet above the finished floor. Use a long level, a hydrolevel, or take measurements up from the floor joists as long as they are all level.

Nail a metal molding strip around the perimeter of the basement using the level marks as guides.

Suspend main runners from the floor joists with screw eyes and wire. Space them 4 feet apart.

Fit cross-tees between the runners to complete the grid. Use the slots in the runners for proper spacing.

Slip the ceiling tiles and lighting panels into the framework. The tiles are usually 2 feet by 4 feet and are held in place by their own weight.

Installing a wallboard ceiling

A conventional wallboard ceiling can be suspended below pipes and duct work, if there is enough headroom. It does not allow access to the utility lines, but it makes a smooth, continuous ceiling possible.

Insulate, as described above. Nail 2 by 4s around the walls at the height of the finished ceiling.

Install a new 2 by 4 ceiling joist below each floor joist. Use plywood scraps or 2 by 4 cleats to connect them, spaced 24 inches apart.

Install light fixtures. Attach wallboard, tape, and finish the joints.

Framing around ductwork. If you are installing a conventional ceiling of wallboard nailed directly to the floor joists, you may have to conceal ducts or utility lines by boxing them in. There should be at least 80 inches of headroom below the box.

Construct the two sides of the framework on the floor. For a long duct, build the framework in sections and splice them together after installing them. Lift them into position and nail them to the floor joists.

Nail crosspieces between the bottom plates of the sides.

Attach the wallboard and tape and finish the joints.

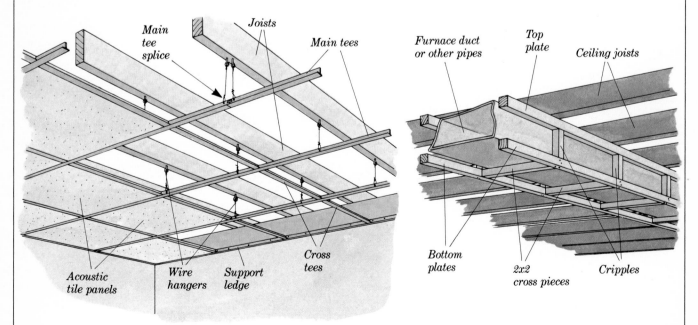

Suspended ceiling

Main tee splice — Joists — Main tees — Acoustic tile panels — Wire hangers — Support ledge — Cross tees

Framing ductwork

Furnace duct or other pipes — Top plate — Ceiling joists — Bottom plates — 2x2 cross pieces — Cripples

Finishing the walls

You can leave masonry or concrete walls exposed or cover them with special waterproof coatings or paints. There are also plaster mixes available that create a waterproof and durable textured coating. However, it is generally desirable to cover the basement walls with wallboard or paneling. The advantages are twofold: improved appearance and insulation.

If the concrete or masonry walls are in good condition, attach finish materials directly to them. If they are rough, uneven, or not plumb, build a false stud wall in front of them. This way you can use fiberglass blanket insulation, which is less expensive than rigid foam panels. This type of wall will reduce both the length and width of the room by about 1 foot.

Attaching to masonry

Make sure any moisture problems are completely solved. Also, if you live in termite country, consult with an exterminator about applying pesticides.

Clean the walls thoroughly to remove dirt and any loose paint. Then remove any trim or moldings around windows and doors. Caulk the joint between wall and floor, and coat the wall with a masonry sealer. Use a sealer that is compatible with the insulation adhesive.

Using wood furring strips the same thickness as the rigid insulation panels, cut pieces to fit the top and base of the wall, around windows, and in corners. Apply construction adhesive to the backs of the furring strips and nail them in place using concrete nails or a stud driver (powder-actuated fastening tool).

Install all electrical wiring, then attach insulation panels horizontally, starting at the bottom. The manufacturer's instructions usually specify applying adhesive to the panels in

Wallboard on masonry

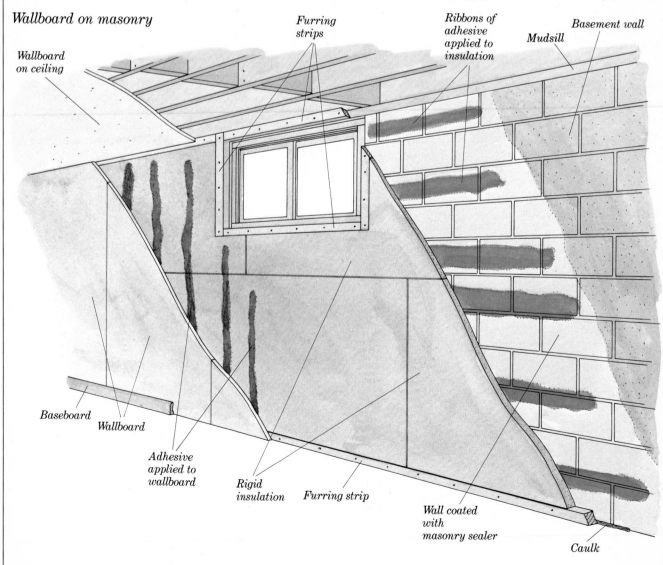

Furring strips

Ribbons of adhesive applied to insulation

Mudsill

Basement wall

Wallboard on ceiling

Baseboard

Wallboard

Adhesive applied to wallboard

Rigid insulation

Furring strip

Wall coated with masonry sealer

Caulk

ribbons, sticking the panels to the wall, removing them for a few minutes, and reapplying them.

Fit the panels tightly together, staggering vertical joints. Score panels with a utility knife and snap them to make cuts.

Do not insulate over water pipes or they might freeze. Try to place loose insulation behind them. Fit the rigid panels tightly against them. Use foam insulation from a spray can to seal any openings not covered by the rigid panels.

Foam insulating panels are flammable. Keep them away from flues. Use fire-resistant fiberglass instead.

Installing wallboard

Install wallboard panels vertically. Use ½-inch-thick panels for a painted wall, ⅝-inch-thick panels if you plan to cover them with wall paneling.

Apply wallboard adhesive to the backs of panels, place them in position, and nail the top and bottom with wallboard nails spaced approximately 7 inches apart.

Cover exposed wallboard edges around windows and at corners with metal edge strips.

Provide access panels for all shut-off and drain valves, cleanout plugs, meters, and electrical junction boxes

by cutting an opening into the wallboard. Cover with a plywood panel cut slightly larger than the opening.

Tape the wallboard joints and finish the walls as desired.

Building a false wall

If it is not feasible to attach materials directly to the masonry walls, build a stud wall in front of them. This type of wall is sometimes used to conceal moisture problems, but it will only forestall, not eliminate, them. They should be solved beforehand.

Framing the wall

The wall can be framed using standard stud-wall framing techniques, with the following differences.

☐ Cover the foundation wall with a plastic moisture barrier stapled to the mudsill. Cut the sheets long enough so that they will lap under the soleplate of the new wall.

☐ Use a single top plate. Nail the top plate to the floor joists above with 16 penny (16d) nails.

☐ If the foundation wall is out of plumb or not flat, use shim stock or 1 by 2 blocks behind the wall.

☐ If there are pipes that run along the foundation wall, attach 1 by 2 or 2 by 4 blocks to clear them.

☐ Use pressure-treated 2 by 4 lumber for the soleplate.

☐ If the floor is concrete, attach the soleplate with 2-inch concrete nails, lag screws and lead anchors, or powder-actuated fasteners 16 inches on center. If fastening the soleplate to a new subfloor, 10d nails are sufficient.

Installing insulation

Staple fiberglass blankets between the studs. Insulate above the top plate in the space between the floor joists.

If there are pipes behind the walls, insulate behind and beside them. Do not let the insulation separate the pipes from the heated space.

Install a vapor barrier over the insulation, if required. Nail wallboard to the studs and finish as desired.

False wall

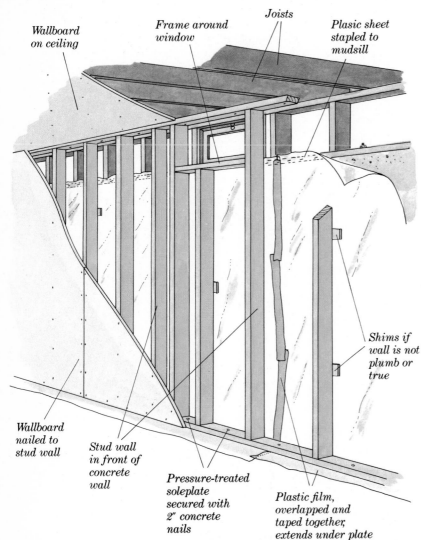

Wallboard on ceiling

Frame around window

Joists

Plasic sheet stapled to mudsill

Shims if wall is not plumb or true

Wallboard nailed to stud wall

Stud wall in front of concrete wall

Pressure-treated soleplate secured with 2″ concrete nails

Plastic film, overlapped and taped together, extends under plate

Installing windows

Adding or enlarging windows in a basement is usually more complicated than it is upstairs. Any opening in the foundation wall is a serious structural change that should be attempted only with the advice of a competent architect, engineer, or builder. It is safer and easier to lower the sill rather than to widen the window. If you lower the sill the header does not have to be changed. Widening a window requires specialized tools and techniques and is not a casual weekend job. However, you may be able to excavate for the light well or perform the finishing operations if you are not able to perform all the following steps.

Shore up any floor joists that terminate above the new window.

Excavate a new light well outside the basement wall. Be sure to provide a drain and build a retaining wall for the light well.

Breach the concrete or masonry basement wall. Add a header the correct size for the total floor and roof area that are bearing on it. Install the header across the top of the window opening.

Install the window frame in the opening and patch around it filling any cracks with mortar. Then install the window in the frame.

Attach trim around the window or leave the edge of the frame exposed to be covered with wallboard.

Finishing a window

Basements present some unique finishing challenges for windows. The thick walls tend to make windows feel smaller. The high placement of most windows can interfere with a suspended ceiling. The outside window well has a strong impact on the view. These finishing techniques can minimize such problems.

Edge transitions. Instead of squaring off the window frame, bevel the inside edge to make a wide frame and reveal more of the window surface. Experiment carefully with the size of the bevel to avoid the mistake of calling too much attention to a small window. For a beveled edge:
☐ Nail or screw cant strips around the window frame. The angle will vary with site conditions, but is usually 10 to 30 degrees.
☐ Bevel furring strips and nail them around the window at a distance determined by the angle of the bevels.
☐ If you are building a false stud wall build a frame of 2 by 4s with beveled edges between the studs.
☐ Insulate and cover with wallboard.

Alternate detail. Instead of a beveled frame, use a stepped frame for the same effect. Frame in two or three steps using progressively thicker furring strips or stud material.

Window well. A terraced window well is much easier to build than a concrete retaining wall, is more attractive than a prefabricated steel liner, and creates opportunities for a miniature garden. Many designs are possible, including the following.
☐ Excavate the soil back away from the well at an angle of no more than 45 degrees.
☐ Install a drainpipe and a drain in the bottom of the well.
☐ Cover the bottom of the well with gravel or concrete.
☐ Build a series of small retaining walls, starting with the bottom one. Make them out of concrete blocks, bricks, timbers or wide boards, and hold them in place with pipe stakes or galvanized steel plates.

Beveled window in a light well

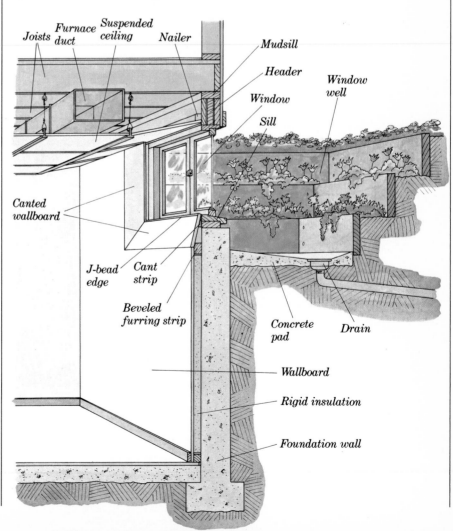

Creating an outside entrance

An outside entrance enhances any basement and is well worth the effort to build it. The most difficult step is breaching the basement wall, especially if it is reinforced concrete. In that case it is better to have the wall cut by a professional concrete sawing contractor. You can rent a roto-hammer or jackhammer to help you break through other types of walls.

Building the areaway. Although you only need enough space for a set of stairs, build as large an outside areaway as you can. It will make an extra window possible and create a more pleasant entry. A large, ter-raced opening creates a feeling of luxury and is not as difficult to build as an areaway with retaining walls, but if you do not have the space you can follow this procedure for a steep-walled entry.

Excavate a hole large enough for the areaway plus retaining walls, to a depth 4 inches below the foundation floor. If you plan concrete steps,

leave a ramp along one edge of the hole on which to pour the steps.

Dig footing trenches for the retain-ing walls 16 inches wide to a depth that matches the foundation footings.

Set two horizontal rebars in the trench, at least 3 inches from the soil. Pour a concrete footing 8 inches deep in the trench. Install vertical rebar in the wet concrete if it is required for the retaining walls.

Install a drainage line around the exterior of the footing and tie it into the main foundation drain.

Build a concrete block wall to grade level or slightly higher. Start at the corners and fill in between.

Apply waterproofing to the outside surface of the block wall. Use asphalt emulsion, bentonite, a rigid mem-brane, or another method recom-mended for local conditions.

Breaching the foundation wall. Mark cutting lines on the inside of the basement wall for a hole large enough for the doorway and frame. Starting from the inside should re-duce rubble in the basement.

Shore up floor joists for any open-ing wider than 3 feet, or as necessary.

Break through the wall with power tools, hammer and chisel, or sledge-hammer. Make the edges as clean and smooth as possible.

Installing the door. Position an ex-terior door frame into the opening. Temporarily brace it after making sure it is plumb and level.

Fill the area between the frame and the wall with cement mortar or con-crete topping before installing the door in the frame.

Building the stairs. Because of possible weather exposure and the need for a fire escape, the stairway should be concrete, masonry, or steel prefabricated for exterior use.

Concrete and masonry stairs can be incorporated into the retaining walls. Leave a wide ramp along one wall as you excavate and build the stairs on top of it, using standard forming techniques for concrete stairs. Prefabricated steel stringers are available for basement entrances; installation instructions are included.

Covering the areaway. For an all-weather entrance, cover the stairway with a hatch door or shelter. A pre-fabricated greenhouse makes an at-tractive entry and provides extra light to the basement.

For either type of enclosure, form and pour a concrete cap on top of the block retaining walls. The final height depends on the height needed for the stairs and the type of enclosure.

Completing the project

Completing a basement conver-sion—building partition walls, hang-ing doors, finishing the walls and ceiling, installing trim and fixtures, and covering the floor—follows the same procedures as any other room. It is also the stage of construction that seems to last forever. But if your preparation is thorough and your commitment strong, you will be ready. Then you will not only have new living space for your home, but you will also have the pride and satisfaction of having taken a major part in the improvement.

Outside entrance

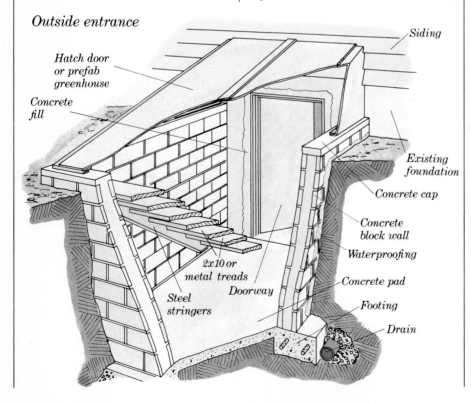

Hatch door or prefab greenhouse

Concrete fill

Siding

Existing foundation

Concrete cap

Concrete block wall

Waterproofing

2x10 or metal treads

Doorway

Concrete pad

Steel stringers

Footing

Drain

INDEX

U.S. Measure and Metric Measure Conversion Chart

		Formulas for Exact Measures			Rounded Measures for Quick Reference		
	Symbol	When you know:	Multiply by	To find:			
Mass (Weight)	oz	ounces	28.35	grams	1 oz		= 30 g
	lb	pounds	0.45	kilograms	4 oz		= 115 g
	g	grams	0.035	ounces	8 oz		= 225 g
	kg	kilograms	2.2	pounds	16 oz	= 1 lb	= 450 kg
					32 oz	= 2 lb	= 900 kg
					36 oz	= 2 1/4 lb	= 1000g (a kg)
Volume	tsp	teaspoons	5.0	milliliters	1/4 tsp	= 1/24 oz	= 1 ml
	tbsp	tablespoons	15.0	milliliters	1/2 tsp	= 1/12 oz	= 2 ml
	fl oz	fluid ounces	29.57	milliliters	1 tsp	= 1/6 oz	= 5 ml
	c	cups	0.24	liters	1 tbsp	= 1/2 oz	= 15 ml
	pt	pints	0.47	liters	1 c	= 8 oz	= 250 ml
	qt	quarts	0.95	liters	2 c (1 pt)	= 16 oz	= 500 ml
	gal	gallons	3.785	liters	4 c (1 qt)	= 32 oz	= 1 l
	ml	milliliters	0.034	fluid ounces	4 qt (1 gal)	= 128 oz	= 3 3/4- l
Length	in.	inches	2.54	centimeters	3/8 in.		= 1 cm
	ft	feet	30.48	centimeters	1 in.		= 2.5 cm
	yd	yards	0.9144	meters	2 in.		= 5 cm
	mi	miles	1.609	kilometers	2-1/2 in.		= 6.5 cm
	km	kilometers	0.621	miles	12 in. (1 ft)		= 30 cm
	m	meters	1.094	yards	1 yd		= 90 cm
	cm	centimeters	0.39	inches	100 ft		= 30 m
					1 mi		= 1.6 km
Temperature	°F	Fahrenheit	5/9 (after subtracting 32)	Celsius	32°F		= 0°C
					68°F		= 20°C
	°C	Celsius	9/5 (then add 32)	Fahrenheit	212°F		= 100°C
Area	in.^{2}	square inches	6.452	square centimeters	1 in.^{2}		= 6.5 cm^2
	ft^2	square feet	929.0	square centimeters	1 ft^2		= 930 cm^2
	yd^2	square yards	8361.0	square centimeters	1 yd^2		= 8360 cm^2
	a	acres	0.4047	hectares	1 a		= 4050 m^2